The DREAM TRAVELER'S QUEST

-1-
INTO THE BOOK OF LIGHT

TED DEKKER
KARA DEKKER

ISBN 978-0-9968124-6-7

Asher Brox's words replayed in Theo's mind. "You show your face in my hall tomorrow, maggot, and I'll show you pain." Theo lay in his bed—a safe place—eyes glued to the rotating ceiling fan, heart pounding, head resting on the sweat-drenched pillowcase. It wasn't a dream. It was a threat.

Maggot, Theo thought. That's how Asher saw him—a sixth-grade bug to be squashed under the boy's ginormous high-top tennis shoe. Flattened like a packet of mayonnaise on the cafeteria floor. Everyone would call him Theo the Mayo for the rest of middle school. He could hear his classmates' taunting rhyme: *Taay-o the Mayo! Taay-o the Mayo!* At least his name didn't rhyme with *vomit*.

Asher was twice Theo's size, an eighth-grader who claimed his stake on the school and didn't like to be bothered, let alone embarrassed, by a sixth-grader who accidentally bumped his tray, spilling green beans and tater tots on him in front of the entire school at lunch.

Everyone knew not to cross paths with Asher Brox. It had been an accident, but Asher didn't care about accidents. He cared about revenge. As far as Theo knew, Asher had never caused any permanent physical damage.

Not yet.

The words Asher had yelled yesterday across the cafeteria wouldn't go away: "You show your face tomorrow, maggot, and I'll show you pain."

Theo slowly swung his legs over the side of the bed. His eyes met the glowing plastic likeness of a caped man plugged into the far wall—The Vanisher.

Sixth-graders don't need nightlights, he reminded himself. But the truth was, he did. Theo hated the dark. It terrified him—along with heights, small spaces, crowded rooms, throwing up, primates, and a handful of other fears that he usually forgot about until he was in the moment.

That's why Theo sought the nighttime protection of Doctor Victor Ersatz—herpetologist by day, The Vanisher by night. Using his invisibility—a side effect of an experiment gone wrong at the university involving thermoregulation in chameleons and a faulty heat lamp—he could in one night thwart a jewel heist, rescue ten people from a burning building, put a derailed train back on its track, and be home in time to do it all over the next day. He was brave, strong, fearless, and invisible—everything Theo wasn't.

Maggot. The word pulled Theo from the world of The Vanisher and into the thought of Asher's fist punching his face. He had to figure out a way to stay home from school.

Theo surveyed his room, looking for inspiration among his collection of Vanisher comics, chapter books, and superhero action figures. Then he saw it: a poster-sized representation of The Vanisher standing on the roof of City Memorial Hospital.

He crept to his bathroom, pulled open the mirror, revealing the medicine cabinet, and examined his options: toothpaste, children's Tylenol, a thermometer, a box of Band-Aids, Q-tips, and a big white bottle of anti-itching lotion for mosquito bites.

Theo had held the honor of perfect attendance up until last year when he unexpectedly came down with the flu. The episode had left his dad with deep concerns for Theo's immune system and an insistence that Theo stay home from school.

So, he would have to make himself sick. Or at least appear sick.

Theo turned the faucet on hot and let it run. While he waited for the water to heat, he smeared some of the lotion on his face and then studied his work in the mirror. *Too much. I'm going for sick, not a black-haired clown.* Theo quickly smoothed the fragrant cream into his cheeks until his naturally tan skin looked mildly pale. Sick. Perfect.

He picked up the thermometer and placed it under the hot water.

"Dad? I'm not feeling so well," he croaked, hoping he'd said it loud enough for his dad to hear but pained enough to pull off his disguise.

He snatched the thermometer from the sink, turned off the running water, scurried to his room, and jumped back in bed. At the sound of his dad's footsteps coming down the hall, Theo quickly placed the hot thermometer in his mouth, narrowed his eyes, and fell into character.

"Hey, buddy, you look like a ghost." His dad placed a hand on Theo's forehead and glanced down at his ailing son. "Interesting."

Theo forced a shiver and moaned. His dad pulled the thermometer from Theo's mouth and peered at him over it. "That high, huh?"

"I feel awful, Dad. Think it's the flu or something like that? Could be contagious. I hear it's going around at school."

"Well, we better get you to the hospital right away. I mean, with a temp of 106.6, you might be dying before my very eyes." He took his finger and wiped the thick liquid off Theo's cheek. "Plus, your skin is melting off." He snickered. "I'll have to check the *HMRG* for this one."

His dad was talking about *The Home Medical Reference Guide*, or the *HMRG* as he and his dad had nicknamed it. Theo wished he had thought of it first. The book was their go-to for any possible ailment—headache, toothache, sore leg, sleeplessness, splinter, possible food poisoning, viral outbreak, plague. He could have used it to come up with something much more convincing.

Theo sat up and sighed.

"What's going on, buddy?" his dad asked, sitting next to him on the bed. "Why this show in the morning?"

"Nothing . . ." Theo said, crossing his arms and avoiding direct eye contact with his dad.

"Theodore Remko Dunnery, talk to me." His full name. "Come on, buddy. What's going on?"

Theo took a deep breath and met his dad's eyes. "Asher Brox is going to beat me up if I show my face in school today."

"Brox, huh? Why would he do that?"

"I guess I looked at him the wrong way."

His dad arched his eyebrow.

"Please let me stay home, Dad? One day. I know you have to teach, but I'm eleven, almost twelve. I can stay home alone." Normally he was afraid of being alone, but today he was more afraid of Asher Brox. "I'll stay in my room. Promise."

His dad shook his head. "Sorry, I can't let you stay, buddy. You know how I feel about your education."

"I know . . . educated people are safe people."

"That's right. Besides, you'll be fine. Now get ready for school. We leave in fifteen minutes."

His dad rose from the bed and started toward the door.

"Dad? Please let me stay? Just this one time?"

His dad turned back. "It's okay to be afraid. Follow the school rules and you'll be fine. That's what the rules are for, to protect us." He smiled. "Besides, you're safer with me. Now, get dressed. Pronto."

Theo pulled on a single-pocket T-shirt, blue jeans, red socks, and a pair of black Converse. Then he looked in the mirror and frowned. Why did he have to be such a wimp?

He finished his morning routine: brushed his teeth, combed his hair, put on deodorant—his dad insisted sixth grade wasn't too early to start—and then headed down the stairs.

His dad was ready and waiting with cinnamon Pop-Tarts on paper plates and lunches packed. "Don't forget your backpack. It's not too heavy, is it? I read an article the other day about heavy backpacks and preadolescent spine development."

"It's fine."

Theo tossed his pack into the back seat of the car and slid into the passenger seat beside his dad.

"Seat belt, buddy?"

Theo stared out his window and watched the houses and trees passing by. "Check."

He imagined himself as The Vanisher running beside them, bouncing off roofs, swinging from trees, balancing on telephone wires. He imagined spreading his cape, catching the wind to keep up with the speeding car. It was a trick his mom had taught him to do to keep calm when he felt like the world was crashing around him. She had known all about The Vanisher because she'd known everything about Theo—all his thoughts, all his interests, all his fears. But he wasn't The Vanisher, and The Vanisher wasn't going to protect him from Asher. Neither was his mom.

It had been two years since she'd died. The brain and lung damage from her car accident had been too much.

"Theo?" His dad's voice shook him from his musing. "You okay?"

"Yeah. Just zoned out."

"Hey, buddy, everything's going to be okay. We've talked about this before. Remember what I've told you."

"There's no need to stand out in the crowd. If they can't find you, they can't hurt you."

"That's right. Stay invisible, Theo, and Asher won't hurt you. It's how I made it through middle school . . . and high school."

"It's a little hard sometimes since we go to such a small Christian school, Dad. And there's lunch, and I have to pass through the eighth-grade hall to get to art, and . . ."

"I know." His dad sighed. "There will always be bullies, Theo. Bullies prey on the small. It's what they've done since the beginning of time. It's a part of life. You can't help that you're small. So, the best thing to do is stay out of their way."

True enough.

Still, it was unfair that Asher never got in trouble for bullying kids at school. The teachers looked the other way to keep their jobs because Asher's father also happened to be the principal. Not only that, but he was nearly as much of a bully as Asher. At least that's how Theo saw it.

Following his own advice to keep clear of any trouble, his dad didn't eat in the teachers' lounge, he never went to the office unless he was called, and he avoided the principal like Theo avoided the monkey house at the zoo.

His dad pulled into the school parking lot and then put the car in park. "I have an idea. How about we hit the comic book shop after school? See what's new?"

The only word Theo heard was "hit," and it further confirmed what was to come: Asher. He nodded, forced a smile, climbed from the car, slung his not-too-heavy backpack over his shoulder, and started walking.

Stay invisible. The grocery store is a few blocks south. I could spend the day there . . .

Then again, if his dad found out he'd skipped school, not only would he be grounded from video games for the rest of his life, but he would receive an hour lecture on the dangers of going to the store alone—dangers like possible kidnapping, jail time, broken bones, contracting incurable illnesses.

Besides, who was Theo kidding? He was too afraid of skipping school and running off by himself. Theo had no choice now but to try to stay invisible.

But how do you stay invisible from someone who is most likely hunting you down?

"Don't worry, Asher's bark is bigger than his bite. Stay invisible. Okay?"

"Okay," Theo said. But he knew it wasn't going to be okay. He appreciated his dad's attempts to connect on his level, but the attempts didn't stop the thoughts from invading his mind.

Maggot.

Theo opened the double doors. The hall was empty with the exception of a few other teachers' kids who had to arrive early.

He exhaled in relief.

Theo grabbed what he needed from his locker and headed to his classroom. Mrs. Baily, Theo's favorite teacher, was there as always, preparing the day's lesson. He looked forward to her class—not that sixth-grade language arts was his favorite, however he loved to read. Mrs. Baily challenged him to dig deeper—understand the words, discover what the author was really trying to say—and she never made him feel dumb for not knowing an answer.

"Hello, Theodore. Early as usual." She peeked over her shoulder and then returned to the dry-erase board. "I've got new books on the shelf, just for you. I figured those old ones were getting a little dull."

"Thanks, Mrs. B."

"Anything for my early bird!"

Theo made his way to the back of the room and plopped down at his desk, thankful for this hour where he didn't have to worry about Asher, but praying for the day to end quickly, even though it had hardly begun. Because when the bell rang, Asher would be in the hall—somewhere among the horde of other eighth-graders—looking for him. How was Theo to stay invisible on his way to his second-hour art class?

Maggot.

Theo controlled his breathing, in and out, trying to calm himself.

"Good morning, Mrs. Baily." Annelee White stepped into the classroom. Theo hardly knew Annelee, but he liked her. There was something about Annelee that made him momentarily forget his fear, but then his thoughts were back on Asher.

Student after student filed in until all the metal desks were full. Theo didn't hear the morning announcements and only caught bits and pieces of Mrs. Bailey's instruction on proper use of pronouns.

Stay invisible.

How? Walk around with a book in front of my face all day?

No, you can't hide being small.

Pass out from the odor of the obviously deodorant-free kid sitting next to me and sleep in the nurse's office?

Nah.

Pretend I have the stomach flu and spend the day in the bathroom stall?

Nope. Pretending to throw up was as bad as throwing up.

But the bathroom wasn't such a bad idea. There was plenty of light, not too small—smelled a bit, but he would deal with it for the short amount of time he planned to be there. He'd leave class early and hide in the bathroom until second hour, then show up late to his next class. They would count him as tardy, but he wouldn't be absent. It could work! It was definitely better than Asher finding him in the hallway.

Theo watched the clock on the wall tick past the minutes of class while Mrs. Baily went on about *The Hobbit*. He had already read it three times and seen the movie.

Stay invisible.

When there were only five minutes left in the period, and Mrs. Baily paused somewhere between Bilbo and the Shire, he lifted his hand.

"Yes, Theo?"

"May I use the restroom?"

Mrs. Baily cast a glance at the clock, hesitated, and then nodded. "Be quick. I'm about to give homework."

Theo stepped up to the front of the class, passed Annelee, grabbed the giant block of wood with the word "BATHROOM" carved into it, and slipped out into the hall.

Empty. His plan would work. Asher and his goons never went to the boys' bathroom in the sixth-grade hall. What eighth-grader would? Besides, everyone in school knew those boys staked their claim on the boys' locker room in the gymnasium.

Theo's sneakers squeaked as he turned the corner. The bathroom was in sight—just a few more steps and then freedom until the tardy bell rang. Safety was so close. He picked up his pace. The plan was perfect; he could come to the bathroom before and after lunch too. Asher would never see him today.

Stay invisible.

His dread of the day began to melt away.

"Hey, maggot!" The voice cut through the silence, sending chills down Theo's spine.

Asher.

"If it isn't my favorite little bug. Didn't I tell you not to show your face today?"

Theo slowly turned toward Asher. The bully towered over Theo with hands the size of basketballs and more facial hair than any eighth-grader Theo had ever seen. He was a middle-school anomaly, a teenager in the body of a man, a replica of his father, Hank, in high-top tennis shoes and a football jersey for a team Theo had never heard of. And now the anomaly stood ten feet away, glaring at Theo.

Maybe he could reason with Asher. "I thought since this is the sixth-grade hall, I . . . I . . ."

"They're all my halls, maggot," Asher growled. "Wasn't very smart of you to show up today, was it? I warned you. So now you know what comes next." Asher's long legs clomped forward, hands balled into fists.

Theo's feet wouldn't move.

"You know, I'm a man of my word. I never break a promise." The bully grinned, exposing a chipped front tooth.

This was one of those moments, those crashing-world moments he and his mother had talked about. He tried to imagine himself as The Vanisher, but all he saw was Asher's fist raring back.

The second-hour bell rang, freeing Theo's mind and then his feet. He spun around and ran. Asher's feet stomped behind him as classroom doors flung open and students eagerly moved from one class to the next. But Theo did not stop, neither did Asher.

Theo rounded a corner, pushing his body harder than he ever had in gym class. The cafeteria doors were in sight. If he could just pass through those doors and fall into the arms of some unsuspecting lunch lady, maybe then he would be safe. Surely Asher wouldn't hit a woman in a hair net? Theo wouldn't put it past him. He had heard worse rumors.

Theo held his breath, pumping his arms, bathroom key securely in his left hand. Theo stopped short in front of the cafeteria, no longer hearing the pounding of Asher's feet on the tile. Carefree students moved back and forth through the halls, closing lockers, carrying books.

Where was Asher?

It didn't matter. Theo was too afraid to go back and look. He needed to sit, to think. He pushed open the cafeteria doors and ran straight into Asher's goons: Thomas Magee, buzzed head and a toothy grin; Billy Kirby, red-headed, smelled like cheeseburgers; and Philip Carter, lanky, freckled, and hadn't paid for his lunch since the first day of seventh grade—he had a way of making others pay.

They were all here. For him. Theo glanced over his shoulder, thinking he should run back the way he'd come. But Asher was now leaning against a locker behind him, hitting his fist repeatedly into his hand.

"Hold him, boys!"

Thomas and Philip grabbed Theo's arms and held him tight. Asher pushed himself off the locker, stepped forward, and paced in front of Theo.

"You make this so easy, you know, like catching a mouse with broken legs. It might be more fun if you made it more of a challenge."

"It *would* be more fun," Billy snarled, circling around Theo like a hungry hyena.

"Was I asking you, doofus?" Asher snapped. Billy cowered.

Asher planted his feet in front of Theo, cocked his head, and glared at him with mocking pity.

"You know this is your own doing, maggot. If you weren't so easily scared, this wouldn't be any fun. But you're always going to be the scared little twerp who hides in the bathroom."

It was as if Asher had uncovered his secret plan. Theo's stomach churned a mixture of Pop-Tart and nerves. Prickles of anxiety climbed up his neck. Terror forced tears to pool in his eyes.

"Please, Asher," Theo breathed. "I tried, but my dad made me come."

"Did you hear that boys? His daddy made him come. You know what my dad always says? Do you?"

Theo shook his head.

"He says there's only one way to toughen up sniveling maggots like you . . ." Asher pulled back his fist and slammed it into Theo's nose. Theo's head snapped back, pulling him to the floor. "I just did you a favor."

Theo gasped for air. Asher and his goons came back into focus, pointing and laughing. Pain radiated behind his eyes and across his face. He lay on the floor like a stuffed doll, waiting for someone to kick him.

Theo forced himself to roll to his side—the tile floor cool on his throbbing cheek. He blinked, focusing on the double doors. He couldn't stay on the floor; Asher would hit him again.

Sucking in as much air as he could, Theo heaved himself off the floor and staggered forward. He crashed through the double doors, followed by footsteps and more taunting laughter.

"Go ahead and try to get away, you sniveling maggot!" Asher sneered.

Theo searched for a place to hide among the couple dozen blue picnic style tables. Blood dripped down his lip, splashing to the floor in tiny droplets. Wherever he went, they would follow.

Stay invisible.

The smell of lunch—fried fish sticks—loomed in the air. The kitchen! Safety No . . . too far. They'd have him before he even got close. He could yell. Theo opened his mouth to cry for help, but instead he coughed. He tried again, frantically surveying his options, but nothing came out.

Please, someone help me!

The doors on the opposite side led to the seventh-grade hallway . . . and the library. If he ran, they would run faster. But it was his best chance.

He glanced back with his hand covering his bleeding nose. The goons pointed and mocked. Suddenly, the metal kitchen doors flew open.

Mr. Grauberger glared at Asher, holding a crate of chocolate-milk cartons. The Grauberger easily made the list of people Theo feared in the school.

In fact, Theo often wondered if the Grauberger was a distant relative of Asher's—big hands, excessive facial hair. "Hey! What's going on here?"

Theo didn't wait. Using the Grauberger as his distraction, he ran, pushed through the doors, made a tight right turn, flew past the row of lockers, and burst into the library.

Mrs. Friend, the librarian, shot a look his way, threw her finger over her lips and shushed him.

"Help me!" he whispered.

She stood from her perch behind a stack of to-be-shelved novels, grabbed a tissue from her desk, and handed it to Theo.

He wiped away an escaping tear with the back of his wrist and held the tissue to his nose.

"Are you okay? What happened?"

Theo didn't know whether to nod or shake his head.

"Do you want to talk about it?"

Theo bit the inside of his cheek, eyes cast to the ground. The tissue was blood soaked. He wondered if he needed stitches.

"How about I let you calm down a bit. Catch your breath. Then we'll talk . . . and tell your dad."

His dad? What would he say? He hadn't stayed invisible, but he had tried. His dad wasn't one to be angry, but he would be worried. His dad always worried about him, especially since his mom had gone.

Mrs. Friend pointed to the set of stairs leading to the second level of the library. It was the place no kid really wanted to go—the reference section. She lifted the key hanging ornately from a gold chain around her neck and pressed it into Theo's hand. "Take this key and—"

Voices outside the library interrupted her instructions: "I bet the maggot went in here."

"We should get back to class, Asher."

"Do you know who my dad is?"

"Yah, but—"

"We find him and shut him up."

Hurried, Mrs. Friend whispered, "There's a narrow door that leads to a room where I keep some of my favorite books. You can stay there while I deal with Asher. Now go!"

Theo ran.

Reaching the top of the stairs, he paused to hear Mrs. Friend chastising the boys for barging into the library and for skipping class.

He didn't wait to see if they would heed her correction. Beyond the dictionaries and outdated encyclopedias, Theo found the narrow door. He placed the key in the lock and turned the knob. He carefully opened the door, slid inside, and then closed the door behind him.

Darkness.

Theo tried to calm his breathing as he spread his fingers across the wall, hands shaking, feeling for a light switch. Asher could have found a way into the room for all he knew.

Finally, his fingers located the switch, and he flipped it on. The room came to life and relief washed over him. Safe. Invisible, for the moment.

The room was much larger than Theo expected. Dusty books bound before the age of modern machinery filled ornately carved wooden shelving to his back and sides. There were no windows—the door was the only way in or out. Intrigued, he ran his fingers along the spines and inhaled the musty aroma of Mrs. Friend's favorite books.

Incredible.

For a moment, Theo forgot about Asher, and then the throbbing in the center of his face reminded him. Theo sat down in the back corner, laid his head against a rather soft book, continued to dab at the blood oozing from his nose, and waited as the fear of Asher and his goons replaced the excitement of his discovery.

They would find him. They would find him, and they would destroy him. They would search the whole library until they found the door. The door! Had he locked the door? Could they see the light? Should he turn it off?

Darkness.

No. He needed the light.

Theo shrank back, small and helpless. He'd always been small. Small like a maggot. Maybe Asher was right. If he was strong, he could fight back rather than hide—rather than having to stay invisible.

Theo shifted to squeeze farther into the corner, bumping the shelf on his right. A book fell from one of the shelves above and landed with a slap directly in front of him, open and glowing with light.

Theo swallowed the lump in his throat and leaned forward, blinking away his tears. The pages of the leather-bound book were crumpled and yellowed. Blank—not a single letter or word.

He leaned closer, drawn to the ancient blank page, almost as if this book whispered his name. A small drop of blood slipped from his nose and splashed on the page.

Oh no!

Every time a student checked out a book, Mrs. Friend cautioned, "Books are your buddies, so bring it back better than when you got it."

This room was where she said she kept her favorites. What if this was one of those favorites?

Theo reacted, reaching for the drop of blood to wipe it away. But the moment his finger made contact with the old paper, bright radiant beams of light streamed from the book.

Theo felt a tug, a pull into the light. The room around him vanished, and he was instantly surrounded by the warm white light.

Then there was nothing.

Not the dark. Not the dark. Theo hesitantly opened his eyes, hoping to be anywhere but in the dark—or in front of Asher. Immediately, he shut them.

Too much light!

He opened them, squinting in the light of the sun, hot and blinding. *The sun? Is that the sun?*

Theo allowed his eyes to adjust to the light, casting its brilliance on miles and miles of sand. *I'm in a desert?*

He sprang to his feet, turned to his left and then his right. *It's a dream. It's just a dream.*

Theo plopped back down on the sand, confused. The sand was hot—he could feel it on his hand. Real. He shot back up, dusting the sand from his blue jeans.

"How's this possible? How did I end up here?" Something was wrong. "Mrs. Friend? Dad?" This wasn't right. He was alone, in a desert.

Alone.

"Help!" he cried. Then again, "Help! Is anyone out there?" He tried to calm his rapid breathing and imagine himself as The Vanisher, but all he saw was sand. *You're fine. You're fine. Everything will be okay. This is just a dream.*

But it didn't feel like any dream he'd ever had.

He tried to remember what had happened before he opened his eyes in this desert, but the panic and speculations of the worst—starvation, dehydration, death—clouded his mind. *Think, Theo, think. What happened?*

He'd touched the book, and then he was here. Where was the book?

The silence of the desert denied him an answer. The constant heat of the sun warmed his hair but brought him no comfort. Still, it was just a dream.

With that thought came the sound of flapping from behind, as if a giant bird or dragon was heading toward him. He caught his breath and ran, afraid to look back. But there was nowhere to run. Just sand. Lots of sand.

The sound of the wings grew louder.

"Help me! Somebody, help me!"

The creature was upon him, tackling him to the

ground as Theo cried out. In the cradle of its wings, Theo rolled until he landed flat on his back, staring at the monster sitting on his chest.

Only it wasn't a monster. It was more like a two-foot-tall fluffy white bird. With its wings folded, it looked more like a gigantic, plump bat. It smiled down at Theo, searching him with its soft green eyes.

"Gabil! Get off him! Can't you see he's terrified!" Another bat, shorter and chubbier but with the same green eyes, landed beside them.

"But, Michal, it's another person from the other world! And look, he's so small! Do you think he can see us?"

"Of course he can see you! And feel you. Off!"

The one named Gabil looked at Theo curiously. "Can you see us?"

Theo blinked, then gave a quick nod.

"He can see us!" Gabil cheered.

"I'm sorry for my friend's behavior," the second bat said as he grabbed Gabil and pulled him off of Theo. "He is easily excited."

Theo backed up on his hands and jumped to his feet. "Who . . . Wha . . . What are you?"

"My name is Michal, and this is Gabil. Please do not be frightened. We mean to bring you no harm. We are Roush."

"And we are very friendly!" Gabil said. "Sorry if we scared you. I thought it could be fun to play a game of fly and tag. But then you can't fly, so it would be unfair. Unless you can fly. Oh, can you fly?"

Theo looked at the bat with wide eyes and shook his head slowly.

"Thought so. No wings."

"Gabil," Michal murmured under his breath, "stop overwhelming the child."

"I'm not overwhelming him. I'm simply asking questions."

"Look at his face, white as yours. He's very frightened."

"Why should he be frightened?" Gabil asked. "I am master of the Roush arts. Nothing can touch me, young boy." Gabil flew into the air, kicked out his leg in a rather awkward manner, and punched toward the sky.

Had he not been in shock, Theo might have laughed out loud at the bat's karate demonstration.

Gabil landed before him and bowed. "See, not overwhelming him!" He smirked.

Michal frowned.

Theo could not believe what he was seeing. Talking ninja bats—he'd never read about anything like this. "I . . . I'm dreaming. I must be dreaming."

Gabil cocked his head to the side curiously. "You surely are not dreaming. Do you need me to show you my skills again? You will see that you are not dreaming."

"What's your name, boy?" Michal asked, waddling forward.

"Theo," he stammered.

"Wonderful name!" Gabil said.

"If this isn't a dream, where am I? How did I get here?" Theo asked, realizing the creatures seemed harmless enough.

"We are in one of the many deserts of this world," Michal said. "I won't bore you with the names. You actually landed very close to where we call home. An hour walk to the north and you'll hit our village."

"I don't understand. I was at school and now I'm in a desert speaking with humongous . . . bats!"

"We are Roush, not bats," Gabil said. "And Talya sent us to find you."

"Talya? Who's Talya?"

Gabil looked past Theo, eyes round. He pointed. "Him!"

Theo looked up and saw a man with long white hair and beard riding toward them on a white horse. For a moment, the older man reminded Theo of Gandalf the Grey. Beside him strolled a large lion, eyeing Theo curiously.

Theo casually edged behind Gabil.

"Are you hiding?" Gabil said. "No need to hide."

Talya approached them and slid off his horse. Judah halted beside him and sat down, eyes still on Theo.

"Hello, Theo. I've been awaiting your arrival. The Roush have already told you who I am, or perhaps not." Talya shifted his eyes playfully toward the two Roush. "One can never guess what our talkative Gabil will say." Gabil flew to him and landed on his shoulder, grinning widely.

Talya's brow arched. "If you don't mind, I'm not a tree and you're much too heavy."

Gabil jumped off his shoulder, landed with a thump, and waddled over to Judah. The playful Roush flipped and flopped around, kicking the air, trying to impress the massive creature.

Talya ignored them, keeping his eyes on Theo. "Try to understand, Theo; you were brought here on a quest."

Theo wasn't sure he was hearing this man called Talya correctly. *Me? A quest?*

Talya nodded. "Yes, you, Theo. You are confused and a bit frightened, but there's no need to be afraid. You were meant for this quest. I will send you with this—" he nodded in Gabil's direction and grinned, "with this energetic ball of Roush."

"Truly?" Gabil spun toward them. "Another adventure like with Thomas Hunter?"

An adventure? Thomas Hunter? Dream or not, Theo was positive they had the wrong boy.

"What is our role?" Michal asked, calm and matter-of-fact.

"You will be his guide. Help Theo find his way

to the top of Mount Veritas. He will begin his quest there."

"I've never been to the top of Veritas!" Gabil cried, hopping up and down.

"I would also like you to take one of your students on this quest."

"Really?" Gabil said. "Who?"

"A younger Roush will be good for Theo."

"An apprentice!" Gabil paced, tapping the tip of his wing to his fuzzy chin. "But which one?"

"Anyone you like," Talya said.

It was too much for Theo to take in—the Roush, Talya, a quest. "Excuse me, what if I don't want to go on a quest?"

A hush fell over the Roush. Judah woke from his dozing. Talya looked at Theo. His eyes were kind, accepting, like Mrs. Friend's. "Why on earth would you not want to go?"

"Sir—"

"My name will do."

"Talya, I don't know where I am, who you are, why these bats can talk, why you have a pet lion. I don't know anything!"

Talya stooped over and lifted Theo's chin with his fingers. "You have many questions. Everything will become clear."

He winked, stepped back, and smiled.

"Besides, I do believe it will be the only way out of the predicament you find yourself in with that bully, yes?"

Asher? Talya knew about Asher?

Talya dipped his head. "This quest will save you, Theo. I highly recommend it."

"What quest?"

"The quest to find the five Seals of Truth. It will be the greatest undertaking of your life, that much I can assure you."

"What five seals? What are they made of?"

Talya offered him a slight smile. "The seals are truths, not objects. They will save you from your fears, both in this world and the one you call home."

"So this isn't a dream? I'm in another world?"

"You will see. And now I must be off. I will meet you at the top of the mountain."

Judah rose, shook his mane, and yawned. Then Talya was off, riding away from Theo and the two Roush with Judah trotting close behind.

Talya hadn't answered any of his questions. *You will see.* Theo hoped he would see. In a few hours he'd have to meet his dad to go home from school.

"We'd better be off if we want to make it to the mountain before the sun sets," Michal said, his big green eyes on Theo. "Ready?"

Theo hesitated. "I guess." But he didn't feel ready. Not at all.

Gabil continued with his hopping up and around. "Oh, this is going to be so much fun! I know who we will bring. You will love him! It will be such a wonderful adventure. Dangerous, but I'm the slayer of beasts and your protector."

Theo gulped. Talya hadn't say anything about *dangerous*.

The Roush talked back and forth about seemingly important things, but Theo's mind was too busy thinking about his potentially *dangerous* situation to listen. None of it made sense. He was confused and lost and wanted to be home.

Then again, if home was at school with Asher hunting for him, maybe he wasn't ready to go home. But he wasn't ready for a dangerous quest in a strange world either.

A quest was meant for someone who was brave, strong, fearless—like The Vanisher. Theo wasn't any of those things. Talya must have mixed him up with someone else, because there was no way he should be chosen for a quest.

Theo's stomach grumbled. He should have eaten more than a Pop-Tart for breakfast. Sweat dripped down the sides of his face, forming tiny tracks on his dusty, sun-kissed skin. He thought the Roush said the journey would take an hour, but his feet felt otherwise. "Are we there yet?"

How long had he been gone? Worry crept back in but was immediately cast away when the desert suddenly changed from hot sand to lush green trees and grass.

Gabil turned to the awestruck Theo, excitement in his eyes. "Are you ready? Few humans have ever seen our homes. Few humans can see us anymore, but you—you are very special, Theo!" Gabil took off up into the air and flew away.

"Where is he going?"

"To tell the others you are coming." Michal stopped walking in the middle of the forest where giant trees cascaded over them. He leaped into the air and disappeared into the tops of the trees.

Theo was alone again. "Michal? Gabil?"

Silence.

"Hello?"

"Over here, Theo!" Gabil's voice called down to him.

Theo tilted his head back. "Oh, wow!"

Nestled into the tops of the trees were small tree houses, hundreds of them. The small wooden huts were beautiful, brightly colored, all different shapes and sizes. Little white heads popped out from windows and doors, their green eyes on Theo. Not even in his stories—the ones he read and the ones he imagined—had he seen such a place. And if he had wings and wasn't so afraid of heights, he'd fly to the treetops to take a peek inside the collection of huts.

Gabil swooped down from one of the houses and landed next to Theo. "This is Theo, my new best friend!" he announced so that all the Roush could hear him. "He is brave and kind, so do not be afraid. Talya has sent him."

With this reassurance, the Roush emerged from the concealment of their dwellings and floated to the ground. Some of the Roush hobbled up to Theo curiously, poking him and ruffling his black hair as though they had never seen a child before. Others kept their distance, whispering to each other about the newcomer.

Gabil stood close to Theo, quickly shushing away a gathering of highly curious baby Roush who had started to crawl up Theo's pant legs. "Go. Go. Go! Back! Leave Theo be, you little ones. Go!"

"This way," Gabil said, grabbing Theo's hand, leading him away from the crowd. Gabil showed Theo a stream of water trickling from a spout in a large tree and made him a cup from one of the tree's leaves. "We've had a very long journey, and there is more to come. Drink."

Theo took a big sip from the leaf cup. The water tasted sweet, almost as if his mom's sweet tea flowed from within the tree. He wished she could have seen this place. "Did you put sugar in my water?"

"Sugar? What is sugar?" Gabil asked.

"White powder to make things sweet. You know, sugar."

"White powder like sand? You use sand to make things sweet? You are funny, Theo!" Gabil fell to the ground, rolling around, laughing uncontrollably like a small child.

"No, silly," Theo said. "Sugar."

Gabil stopped his rolling, gazing at Theo, dumbfounded. Then Gabil started up again. Theo burst out, catching the Roush's contagious joy-filled laughter. Theo laughed so hard his sides hurt.

Gabil stood, a bit tipsy in his attempt to compose himself. "I must find Stokes. Wait here; I'll be back."

The Roush sprung into the trees, leaving Theo to wait, alone—again. Suddenly, a swift rustle moved through the trees. Theo saw it—a small Roush was flying at him. Theo ducked, covering his head like he had been taught to do during a tornado drill.

The Roush's feet hit the ground a few inches from where Theo crouched. The small creature attempted to stop but tripped, flew forward, and crashed straight into Theo. They spilled over into the soft grass, making it the second time he'd been tackled to the ground by a fluffy white bat. Although he was quite sure this time was by accident.

"I'm sorry, I'm sorry, I'm so sorry! I didn't mean to knock you over," the smaller Roush cried. "I've been working on my landings. My dear, that wasn't good. Please don't tell Gabil."

The Roush was fluffier than Gabil and Michal. His green eyes protruded from his small white face, and his ears appeared too big for his head. Theo had the sudden urge to scoop the wee-Roush up in his arms—if the ball would sit still long enough. But he refrained.

The Roush offered his small winged hand to Theo. "My name's Stokes!"

"I'm Theo."

"Yes, I know! Gabil told me. I've been chosen to be your protector, and have no fear," he turned his head to one side, then the other, "my friends call me the Shataiki Slayer."

"No, they don't," a Roush chuckled, flying above them.

"Some do!" Stokes called to the passing creature.

"Shataiki?" Theo asked.

"Nasty, fanged, red-eyed black beasties. They fly, like us, but they are much too thin. Not pretty. They have snouts too."

Theo gulped. "Fangs?"

"Yes, long pointy teeth and—"

"Stokes!" Gabil landed next to them, a grin spread across his furry face. "You're here! Good, you've met Theo." He turned to Theo. "I've chosen Stokes to come on the quest with us. He is soon to be a skilled fighter, under my careful instruction, of course."

Stokes bounded into the air and kicked, but as he returned to the ground, his right foot twisted over his left. He tripped and rolled head first into a tree trunk. He popped to his feet and boldly waddled back to them, attempting to cover up his embarrassment with a confident lift of the head.

Gabil chuckled. "He's got some more work to do, naturally, but he's brave."

"Yes, I told Theo not to fear when he is with me," Stokes said, flexing his barely visible muscles.

"Slayer of Shataiki," Gabil said, giving Stokes a wink.

"How are your skills in the Roush art, Theo? I'm sure you're a master too."

Theo bit his lower lip and fiddled with his fingers behind his back. He tried to think how he'd tell them he had never fought anyone before, and he could hardly call his run-in with Asher a fight. Every comic book he had ever read portrayed a fight as a back-and-forth exchange of contact. With Asher there had been no exchanging of anything.

"The truth is, I don't know how to fight."

"Well, then," Gabil cried, "I must show you some simple moves in the Roush fighting art before we begin your quest!" He grabbed Theo's hand. "Follow me!"

Gabil led him deeper into the forest. At the center of a small clearing, someone or some Roush had tied black bats made of straw to long sticks. Their pupil-less red eyes appeared to be made of stones, and their sharp fangs, pieces of tree bark.

Shataiki.

In addition to the straw Shataiki, red-and-white painted targets dotted the open space, staked in the ground and hanging from tree limbs. Stokes took off running, passing Theo. He flew up into the air, pulled his knee to his chest and then thrust it out with his foot flat, slamming into the head of the straw Shataiki. The stick figure crashed backward to the ground, sending pieces of straw flying. The straw Shataiki popped back in place as Stokes landed on the ground, nearly, but not quite, falling over.

"Wow," Theo whispered. "Shataiki Slayer."

"This is where all my students train," Gabil said, evidently pleased by Stokes's show. "I've trained some pretty excellent fighters, if I do say so myself! And now I will train you."

He had often dreamed of being a superhero like The Vanisher—a fighter, a server of justice. But if the Roush were real, then so were those red-eyed beasts. "Train me? No thanks. I think I'll stick with staying invisible."

"Nonsense! You can't be invisible forever. At some point you will have to fight. It's a simple matter of knowing how and when."

"I don't really want to learn to fight right now. Maybe another time," Theo said, eyes on his black Converse.

Just then, Michal soared in and landed beside them. He glanced between Gabil and Stokes with some disapproval. "Theo and I will gather some supplies for our journey."

Gabil nodded, offering Theo an encouraging smile. Theo smiled back and followed Michal away from the training grounds. Neither Michal nor Theo spoke as they walked. Theo followed until Michal stopped next to a tree with two big brown bags at its base.

Supplies, Theo guessed.

"Michal?" Theo asked, staring up at the isolated house perched high in the tree—maybe Michal's.

"Yes?" Michal asked, picking up a bag.

"I think Talya has the wrong person. I thought I

might be the one, but I don't know anything about fighting or going on quests—only what I've read about in books, but those aren't real. If this is real, if it's not a dream and those Shataiki are as scary as they sound—"

"Talya knows and Talya is to be trusted."

"How could he know?"

"He's the grand mystic from the realm of mystics."

"A mystic? Like a magician?"

"Oh no, not magic," Michal said. "A mystic is someone who knows Elyon. Most know *about* Elyon, but they don't truly know him. Mystics do. They are no longer blind, so I'd say that's pretty magical, but not magic."

"And who's Elyon?" The name sent an unexpected rush of energy through Theo. He paused to catch his breath. "Is he . . . a mystic or a Roush?"

"Elyon . . . well, isn't that the mystery the mystics have understood. You will soon understand more about him, but we must begin our journey in order for you to truly know. All will be clear in time, my boy."

"But what about the Shataiki? They have fangs! And Stokes said—"

"Stokes continues to learn. The Shataiki are masters of trickery and deceit, but their true power comes from their lies and your belief in those lies. Know who you are and they are powerless. That is all I will say on the subject of Shataiki. Now grab the bag."

Theo and Michal met Gabil and Stokes at the edge of the Roush village, and together the four began their trek toward the mountain.

"Theo, I was wondering, if not the fighting arts, what do you learn in your world?" Stokes asked as they pressed forward.

"I don't know . . . math, science, social studies, language arts."

"Language arts! That sounds fun! Do you fight with your language?"

Theo laughed. "No, Stokes. We learn how to use words, and we read books."

"Oh! Like the *Book of Histories*!"

Gabil and Michal passed a glance one to another.

"We do have history books, but I prefer comics."

"Comics?" Stokes scratched his head. "Is it a language art too?"

"That's enough questions, Stokes," Michal stated.

A moment of silence passed.

"I started my training with Gabil two years ago," Stokes piped up. "It's quite an honor to be with Gabil. He's a legend."

"Stokes! A few moments of quiet, please. Theo has much to process as it is."

"Hmmm. Seems backward, that's all. Language arts . . . what is the purpose?"

Before long, after more of Stokes's inquisition into the life of Theo Dunnery, the quartet stood at the base of the mountain. Theo stared up at the lush, towering peak in front of them, noticing the stairs carved deep into its side.

Without questioning, Theo followed Michal—silent at the head of the crew—occasionally glancing above him for the winged red-eyed Shataiki. Play-by-plays of what the beasts might do to him occupied his thoughts, so much so that he found himself completely blocking out the excited chatter of Stokes.

"We are almost to the peak!" Michal called back to the party.

Theo stopped to catch his breath in the thinning air. His feet ached, feeling every pebble and stone through the white rubber of his tennis shoes. The backs of his legs seemed to have developed a pulse, but mostly he was exhausted and wanted to curl up in his bed.

They'd climbed halfway up the mountain when Michal finally stopped at the mouth of a large cave.

"There it is!" Gabil shouted. "There it is!"

Inside the cave, two giant wooden doors towered before Theo and the three Roush. Michal lifted his white wing and knocked three times. The banging vibrated all around them. The doors opened, revealing a pathway leading deep into the mountain.

Pale light flickered from fire-lit torches lining the walls. The concept of an unwelcome wind extinguishing the flames and leaving the travelers in complete darkness frightened Theo.

He looked over to Stokes, whose round eyes bulged, searching the uncertainness of the tunnel. Was Stokes the Shataiki Slayer afraid too?

The path opened up into a room no bigger than Theo's bedroom at home. Five arched wooden doors adorned the wall in front of him—each a different color and each with a different symbol carved into the cave wall above it.

The first door was white with a large white hollow circle above it. The next door was green, and above it another hollow circle, however this circle was green and a bit smaller than the white one.

A black door stood beside the green, and on its other side a red door. Above the black door was a solid black circle, and above the red, a red cross. On first sight, Theo thought the fifth door was a repeat of the first—white. But above was a single white dot.

"My friends, you made it just in time," a voice said behind them.

Theo turned to find Talya standing at the entrance of the room.

He winked at Theo. As if on command, two torches came to life beside the first door, their flames dancing against the rock wall.

"Theo Dunnery," Talya said as he walked toward them, stopping next to Theo, "here before you are five doors. Behind each door you will discover one of the five Seals of Truth. At your quest's end, you will know all five seals. But in order for the quest to end, it must begin with the first: white. Find the lake, find the seal, and you will begin to find the courage you seek."

Begin to find courage? How long will it take to actually conquer my fears?

"As long as it takes to find all five seals," Talya said. There was that thing again where Talya knew Theo's thoughts. "The lake is a two-day journey once you pass through the door. Follow the river until it meets the edge of the forest. The trees will give way to sand and there you will find a cavern. It is past that cavern where you will find the lake."

River. Forest. Desert. Cavern . . .

"Do not worry, Theo. The Roush will remember the way, but do take care to avoid trouble."

Trouble?

"I don't think I'm ready," Theo said, backing up.

"You would not be here if you were not ready."

"Everything will be fine," Stokes said, grabbing Theo's hand. "I'm a little nervous too—this is my first time away from the Roush village. But Gabil will protect us all." And then he added, "And I'll protect you too."

"Place your hand on the door, Theo," Talya instructed. "It responds only to you."

"Me?"

"It's your quest."

Stokes nudged Theo forward with the tip of his wing.

Theo took a deep breath and stepped toward the door. He lifted his hand and placed it on the white wood. "Here goes nothing."

With a gentle push, the door opened, and a burst of light exploded from the other side, pulling Theo and the three Roush through, exactly as the book in the library had done.

Theo landed with a thump. He scrambled to his feet and surveyed the area. Michal, Gabil, and Stokes were sprawled out on the river bank, struggling to get up.

Theo waved his hand back and forth through the air, searching for the door. "Where did it go? It disappeared. How did it do that?"

"It is the mystery of Elyon," Michal said as if doors appeared and disappeared every day.

"What if we want to go back?" Theo asked.

Michal looked at him matter-of-factly. "We don't."

Stokes flew up into the air and flipped forward. "Can you believe it? My very first mission!" He hooked his leg in a powerful kick to the right, followed by a double backflip and a side kick to the left. Gabil shot up to his protégé, demonstrating and instructing a series of maneuvers that rivaled anything Theo had read about The Vanisher.

They don't seem worried. "Maybe this won't be so bad," Theo said to Michal.

"Maybe." Michal waved at the two in the sky. "All right, come on, you two. There's no time to dally about."

Stokes plopped to the ground next to Theo, wrapping his wings around him. "I am honored to be here with you, Theo of Dunnery. Let's make this an adventure we will never forget!"

Theo had to admit, traveling through beams of light was exciting. If he could somehow master that mystery, Asher would never be a problem—especially if Theo could learn to stick the light-travel landings. "Yes! An adventure we will never forget!"

The river quickly gave way to the forest where tall trees reached for the sky with vibrant leaves dancing in the wind. Shafts of sunlight peaked through the branches, landing on Theo's arms, warming him, comforting him. And the wind was sweet, kind of like the water Gabil had given him.

He had three new friends, two guides and a protector, walking in front of him on their way to the lake. He had never really had friends before. Now, he not only had friends but talking, fighting, mysterious creatures as friends! No one would believe big white bats talked to him in a world of mystics and vanishing doors.

He, Theo Dunnery, was on a quest. It was too good to be a dream—perfect, safe. If he could stay here forever, he'd never have to see Asher Brox again. He wondered what was happening in his world. Did his dad know he was gone? Was he worried? What if the school was on lockdown? They'd search the lockers for sure—sixth-graders wound up in lockers all the time. Could he be stuffed in a locker and not know it?

"Um, Michal, I'm at school, but I am also here. All this isn't just a dream, right?"

Stokes stopped short directly in front of Theo. "Can you not see us?"

What was it with them and being seen? "Of course I can see you."

Theo needed answers, especially if his dad thought he was missing. His dad would be a frantic mess. "I guess I'm asking, what's happening to me in my world?"

"Well, we don't know. See, we've never been to your world," Michal said.

"Oh."

"Gabil!" Stokes cried, bouncing up and down. "Tell Theo the story of when you singlehandedly defeated those forty Shataiki!"

"Forty, Gabil?" Michal asked, eyeing him. "That seems a bit of a stretch."

"Perhaps it was a smaller number, but it doesn't change the fact that I destroyed them all. There I was in the middle of the desert, alone, when the beasts approached me."

Theo's attention was snatched away by a passing shadow to his right. He turned on his heel. Nothing. Then another shadow formed above him, but when he looked up, he saw branches and leaves.

Theo kept his eyes focused above him. "I don't mean to interrupt your story, Gabil—"

"No, please do," Michal said.

"Did you by any chance see something strange? Like shadows? I'd swear something flew past us."

"Hmm, I didn't see anything, perhaps it was shadows from the trees?" Gabil said.

"Of course you didn't see anything, Gabil," Michal said. "You were too focused on telling your ridiculous story."

"I'll keep my eyes sharp," Stokes said, lunging into a fighting stance. "You point when you see another!"

"There!" Theo yelled, pointing behind Stokes. "Behind those trees! Do you see it?"

Gabil looked then leaped in front of Theo as if to shield him. "Stokes, formation! We are not alone here!"

Stokes's eyes went wide. "Are you sure?"

"Quite. Ready yourself!"

"But—" Stokes took a step backward, "I'm not ready for a real fight yet."

"What do you mean?" Theo asked, backing up with Stokes. "I thought you were a warrior?"

"None of my students have actually seen or fought a Shataiki before," Gabil cried over his shoulder. "But they've trained for the day. Stokes, you will be fine. Remember, we must keep Theo safe."

A twig snapped. Theo jumped.

But there was nowhere to go. Nowhere to hide.

Gabil spun toward the noise and inched forward. "Who goes there? Come forth!"

Theo shivered. The warm air had turned cold. He held his breath, afraid to breathe. In front of him, Stokes shook, equally as terrified. So who was going to protect whom?

"Michal, do you hear anything?" Gabil asked, eyes locked on the forest.

"No. A false alarm, perhaps."

Theo peered into the woods, praying the shadows had been his imagination. But then he saw two red eyes deep within the trees.

Shataiki!

Fear spread through his arms, ice cold. He tried to speak, but nothing came out. Another pair appeared next to the first, and suddenly there were dozens of red eyes glaring at him.

"Gabil?" Theo finally managed, lifting a trembling finger.

The Roush followed Theo's finger to the eyes.

"Stokes, grab Theo and run north toward the desert when I give the word," Gabil whispered.

"What about you and Michal?" Stokes asked.

"Right behind you. But if something happens to us, you must take Theo. Understood?"

"But, Gabil—"

"Get to the desert and follow it north. You'll be fine."

Red eyes began to rise from the trees. The sound of hissing and flapping overpowered the wind. They were coming.

"I think our time has run out," Michal said.

"Now, Stokes!" Gabil cried. "Go!"

Stokes grabbed Theo, pulling him by the arm, and ran. Gabil and Michal were on their heels. The hissing behind him went from a whisper to a full chorus. Theo dared a glance behind and saw a black cloud rising from the tops of the trees, racing toward them.

"There are too many!" Gabil cried, leaping into the air. "Take flight, Stokes! Run, Theo! Run faster!"

Stokes leaped into the air and spread his wings. Their small feet would prove pointless in a race, but they couldn't fly too fast and leave Theo behind.

He ran as fast as he could directly below them, dodging trees and jumping over logs. The ground below Theo's Converse hardened as he pounded forward. The trees no longer felt bright and magical but instead like tall stone pillars that were in his way.

The sound of the hissing seemed to be getting closer!

They broke out of the forest. Theo found himself running on a narrow ridge with a mound of dirt to their right and a valley far below to their left. He feared heights almost as much as he feared the dark, but the Shataiki closing in pushed that fear aside. Where were the random doors and bursts of light when he needed them?

He flashed a look up to see a huge black bat ten feet above him. The sight was so frightening that he stopped dead in his tracks. Its long tongue flickered as it clicked. Piercing red eyes burrowed into Theo. *Shataiki!* More terrifying than he had imagined.

"Michal!" Gabil cried. "They're going after him!"

Theo tore his eyes from the beast and focused

on Stokes, running faster. Shrieks filled his ears as Gabil and Michal tore into the few Shataiki that had reached them.

"Hurry!" Stokes yelped, twisting back. His eyes bugged with fear. "Run!"

Theo glanced up again. One of the black bats was falling from the sky, shredded by Michal. He was so fascinated by the sight of the plummeting beast that he completely lost focus of his feet running below him. His right foot rammed into a rock buried deep in the earth, knocking him off balance.

Stokes dove for him and clasped his shirt, but it was too late. Theo stumbled forward and they both crashed to the ground at the ledge.

The ground along the edge crumbled under the force of their landing. Theo's legs gave way. Stokes desperately tried to pull him back up but he wasn't strong enough.

Theo's arm slipped out of Stokes's grasp. He landed with a thud. Pain shot through his back and legs. It felt as if every nerve in his body was screaming. Theo pulled himself to a sitting position, legs extended in front of him, and forced his eyes to focus on the area around him—another forest, much darker than the one before. Where was Stokes? He spun around, terrified.

"Stokes! Where are you?"

No reply.

"Stokes, please!

Theo's panic escalated. He couldn't get enough air into his lungs and his legs were shaking. Then he heard a noise from the trees in front of him, like the rustling of leaves—like someone or something moving toward him. Theo scrambled to his feet, trying to ignore the pain that rushed through his bones.

"Stokes?" Theo whispered.

"Not . . . t . . . t exact . . . t . . . tly." A Shataiki emerged from the shadows of the trees, red eyes glistening in the light. The Shataiki's mouth pulled to a grin, and Theo saw the bat's sharp fangs drooling with delight. Its filthy black fur was matted and reeked of rotten eggs. The creature's presence loomed over Theo, despite its shorter three-foot stature.

"Th . . . Theo, it's nice t . . . t . . . to finally meet you. My name is Shax. My leader is v . . . v . . . very excited to meet you as well." The creature inched closer to Theo, an eerie hiss hanging with each stuttered consonant.

"Go away!" Theo croaked, backing up.

"Oh, yes that w . . . w . . . would be nice, b . . . b . . . but unluckily for you I'm not very nice."

A cry filled the air: "Kiai!" As if dropped from the sky, a little snowy ball of fur swooped in, colliding with Shax.

Stokes! A rush of relief flooded Theo. His protector was here to save him.

The Roush's foot struck Shax in the face. Shax flailed backward. Stokes jumped on top of Shax, holding him down, but Shax took his feet and slammed them into Stokes's belly. Stokes hit the ground, his white head bouncing off a fallen branch.

"Stokes!" Theo screamed.

Four more Shataiki dropped from their cover among the dense foliage. Two of the Shataiki grabbed Stokes, and the other two worked their way behind Theo. Theo's eyes met Stokes's. Fear and failure filled the childlike green eyes. He knew Stokes was already blaming himself for their capture.

One of the Shataiki slammed a rock on Stokes's head and the Roush slumped over, knocked out cold.

"No! Stop! Stokes!"

One of the Shataiki threw a bag over Theo's head. Darkness. *Not the dark, anything but the dark!*

Theo tried to break free, kicking and throwing his shoulders, but the Shataiki's grip was too strong.

The rope binding Theo's wrists cut into his skin as they jerked him along. He toppled forward, fighting to maintain his balance so as not to do a face-plant on the ground. With every step Theo took, his fear of the unknown grew stronger.

The ground changed from wet grass to hot sand under his shoes. Were they back in the desert where he had first met the Roush and Talya—the desert where all of this had begun? Maybe the Roush and Talya were here, ready to jump out and save Theo and Stokes from the clutches of the Shataiki. But where was Stokes?

The small Roush hitting the branch played over in the darkness. Theo listened to see if he could distinguish Stokes's wobble from the shuffling of Shataiki talons, but all he heard was the crackle of their chatter.

With a jolt to the wrists, Theo's body lurched forward to a halt. The Shataiki stopped. The chatter quieted, replaced by a low hissing. Theo inhaled the scent of burning wood that overpowered the beasts' stench.

Something ripped the bag from his head. Theo blinked, adjusting his eyes to the blazing firelight. The shadows of hundreds of Shataiki lined the ledges of the canyon's towering walls, and he could see a bundle of white fur strung up on a pole.

Stokes!

The Roush's head hung down, his chest slowly lifting up and then falling—unconscious but alive.

Shax stood in front of Theo, a toothy grin plastered across his face. Next to Shax, a larger, bulky Shataiki glared at Theo. Shax lifted his chin, staring up at the large Shataiki. "My s . . . sire, I g . . . g . . . got him," Shax stammered.

"Yes, I see." The bigger one tilted its head, examining his captive with its dark crimson eyes, revealing the long scar dug across its right eye. Theo cringed at the sight of the massive beast, especially the dried blood crusted on his snout. Its overwhelming odor, far worse than the others—dank, sour, pungent—filled Theo's nostrils, making him dizzy and lightheaded.

"Hello, Theo." The creature's gravelly voice rattled

Theo's bones. "I am Ruza, and I've brought you here for a very special reason. Would you like to know what it is?"

Theo opened his mouth to speak, but what he wanted to say wouldn't come out.

"Answer me, please," the leader said. "I asked if you would like to know why I brought you here."

"Shataiki are liars. I shouldn't trust you," Theo stammered.

"Is that what they told you? I'm the liar?" Ruza chuckled, and the hundreds of Shataiki joined in, roaring with heckles and taunts. "You see, my son, the truth is that you've already been lied to. I only want to make sure you get the *truth*. All of what the Roush have told you has been said for their own benefit, not yours. Have they told you about the monster?"

"Monster?" Theo squeaked.

"Elyon. The cruel monster who promises them peace if they become his slaves and follow his commands. And if they don't, well then, they must suffer deeply for a very, very, very long time."

A black fog seeped out of the beast's mouth as he spoke.

"The monster Elyon demands his slaves' perfect obedience. Escaping his punishment is possible only if you believe and do his bidding. He's constantly disappointed by his children's actions, and you don't want to see him get angry. I wouldn't want to be in his line of fire when he blows up."

Asher. It sounded as if Ruza was describing Asher. Could Elyon be like Asher? All Michal and Gabil had given him so far were riddles.

The fog now poured out of the Shataiki's mouth, circling Theo. But Theo barely noticed, too distracted by Ruza's words.

Theo tried to focus on what the Roush had told him. The Shataiki deceive and trick. Michal and Gabil were his friends. "They didn't say Elyon was like that."

"They wouldn't." Ruza placed his black claw on Theo's cheek. "They want you to follow him and become just as deceived as they are. Trust me, boy. They've been lying to you."

"I don't believe you! They're my friends."

"Friends? Who lied to you and brought you all this way to meet a monster they refuse to tell you about? And what kind of friend gives you this pipsqueak of a protector?"

"Don't believe him, Theo." Stokes lifted his head, but it fell back again.

"Pathetic. Do you want to know the truth, Theo? Trust me. I may look nasty, but I would never lie to you."

A high-pitched whistle from Stokes echoed throughout the cavern.

"Silence the Roush!" Ruza ordered. "He calls for help!"

Shax rushed over to Stokes, slapped him across the face, and then gagged him with a piece of cloth.

"Don't hurt him!" Theo snapped.

"Let us help you, boy," Ruza hissed. "Breathe. Breathe in the knowledge held in the fog surrounding you. The knowledge of good and evil is your protector. Breathe and know who this Elyon monster really is. No need to wait and see. You'll understand how evil their master is if you simply breathe."

"I don't know if—"

"Trust me, Theo, knowing the truth is better than confusion. Don't you want to have this knowledge? Knowledge is power."

Stokes shook his head, as if begging Theo not to listen to Ruza. But what if Ruza was telling the truth? What if he had the answer to why Theo was really here? What if Ruza was saving him from the Elyon monster?

"The choice is yours, Theo, but that choice must be made now. Either live in confusion and lies or breathe in the truth. Let all the answers come to you with one deep breath."

"Breathe, breathe, breathe, breathe!" The Shataiki filled the canyon with their voices and slapped their wings against the walls, shaking the very ground beneath Theo's feet.

"Breathe, breathe, breathe, breathe!"

Theo studied the black fog swirling around him. The beating of wings against stone quickened his heart. This was wrong. He had to get far from here. But the Shataiki had defeated Michal, Gabil, and Stokes. They were strong, and Ruza seemed to know lots of things Theo didn't. He knew about the Elyon monster. Maybe he knew how to defeat Asher too.

So, Theo breathed.

The fog flowed through his nose, filled his lungs, and consumed his whole body. Burning pain seared his eyes, and his vision went dark. His arms and legs began to sting, as if the fog flowed through his veins.

Overcome with weakness, Theo dropped to the cavern floor. He barely heard Stokes's muffled screams in the background, begging for him to stop, over the Shataiki's shrieks as they danced in excitement on the top of the walls.

Theo's sight returned, and the pain vanished from his body.

What happened?

"You have inhaled a deeper knowledge of fear. This knowledge of good and evil has blinded you. And I will blind you over and over again, maggot."

Maggot. That's what Asher called him back in the other world!

Ruza chuckled as he lifted into the air.

Shax poked Stokes's cheek with a long skinny finger. "You b . . . b . . . basically handed him over to us. Thanks for your h . . . h . . . help."

In a fit of rage, Stokes threw his head forward and banged it into Shax's forehead.

Shax stumbled back and cried out in pain. "Ouch!"

"Shax, come!" Ruza ordered from the air. "Now!"

"B . . . b . . . but can't I hurt him a l . . . l . . . little more?"

"We've accomplished what was asked of us," Ruza snarled, flying from the canyon.

Shax huffed and took to the air, following the beast.

"Till we m . . . m . . . meet again you filthy Roush slave of Elyon."

The mass of Shataiki trailed after Shax, shrieking cheers of victory throughout the sky. Theo and Stokes were left alone in the canyon—Theo on the ground, too weak to stand, and Stokes tied to the post, gagged.

For a long minute Theo sat immobile, numbed by what had happened.

"There they are!" a voice cried above them. "Elyon help us."

Theo watched with relief as Gabil and Michal landed on the ground.

Gabil quickly unbound Stokes from the ropes and removed the gag from his mouth.

"He let in the black fog!" Stokes cried out, hurrying over to where Michal lifted Theo into the wings of Gabil. "The Shataiki just left."

Michal gave Gabil a worried glance. "He ingested the fog of deception and blindness; there is nothing we can do for him. We must get to the lake as fast as possible."

"I tried to protect him. I am so sorry," Stokes said as he helped Gabil hold Theo.

"It's okay, Stokes. Just help us get him to Elyon."

"I'm so sorry—"

"Enough!" Michal snapped. "We must hurry before he's lost altogether!"

Theo fought to keep his eyes open. He tried to speak to his rescuers but yawned instead—exhausted and weary.

He couldn't stay awake any longer. So he let his eyes fall closed, drifting into darkness.

A familiar aroma stirred Theo's senses. Not the stench of Shataiki or the sweetness of Roush water. It was dusty and aged like . . .

Books!

Theo's eyes shot open. He was back in the library, sitting in Mrs. Friend's room of books.

He was back! He was home! What a dream!

Or was it real?

Theo started to get up but pain coursed through his body. It was worse than the day after the physical fitness test in gym class.

The ancient book lay on the floor, open, baring the stain of Theo's blood. He nudged the front of the book with his foot and lifted the cover. The book plopped shut, sending a small cloud of dust into the air. Somehow he felt better with it closed—and even better after he shoved it back onto one of the shelves. Releasing the book safe into its hold, he noticed his bare wrist. He quickly examined the other.

Rope burn. The Shataiki. All of it, real.

He raced to the door, swung it open, and started down the stairs, but he pulled back when he saw Asher and his goons wandering through the library.

They're here? How is that possible?

He spun on his heels and dashed straight back up to the little room. He closed the door quietly behind him and this time locked it. He pushed the flat of his back against the door, slid down, and sat on the floor.

He had been in the other world for at least a whole day, maybe longer, but here a minute, a blink in time, had passed! He was back in the world of bullies, running away from Asher. But now he knew there was more to fear than Asher Brox, and he had come face to face with one of them.

He'd inhaled the black fog—he could almost feel it crawling up his arms. A shiver passed through him. His arms appeared normal, so that was good, right? But he had breathed it in. It was inside of him. It was a part of him—protecting him with the truth of the monster Elyon. Thankfully, Elyon didn't exist in this world, but Asher did.

The doorknob jiggled. Theo backed away from the door. He'd start throwing books if he had to. Then silence. He waited. He'd been through enough for one . . . minute . . . day. The concept was unbelievable, but the rope burns were real.

A knock startled him.

"Hello, Theo, it's Mrs. Friend. Are you okay in there?"

Theo unlocked the door, stepped out, and handed Mrs. Friend the key. The librarian placed the chain around her neck and with a smile pushed her thick-rimmed glasses up the bridge of her nose.

"They're gone now. I'll have a chat with Principal Brox in the morning. Might not do any good, but I don't appreciate disruption in my library, and I absolutely will not tolerate bullying in any form. You've had a rough morning, Theo. Can I get you anything? An ice pack?"

He shook his head.

"It's okay if you need to hang out here for the rest of your second-hour class."

"Thank you."

"Anything for my favorite student."

He felt himself blush as she turned to leave.

"Mrs. Friend, wait."

Theo slipped back into the little room and

grabbed the leather-bound book off the shelf. He returned and held it out to her.

"Do you know what this is?"

She took the book and looked it over. Then she shook her head and handed it back. "I don't recognize it. But I can honestly say that I haven't read every book in the library. Would you like me to see if it's in the system? You could check it out for a few days and then return it."

"That's okay . . . I don't think I want it."

"Why is that?"

"Just . . . because."

"How about I keep it in here in case you change your mind, that way you'll know where to find it." Mrs. Friend carefully placed the book back on the shelf. "You know, Theo, sometimes the things we need most find us."

Her statement struck him as strange. Odd. Cryptic. Almost like something Talya would say.

"Maybe I should head to the art room. Mr. O'Brian will think I'm skipping class or fell in the toilet or something."

She chuckled and ruffled his hair. "Well, we can't have that, Theo Dunnery. I'll write Mr. O'Brian a note, letting him know you were with me . . . and not in toilet."

For the rest of the day, Theo decided it might be safer to move with the pack of frenzied students between classes—ducking behind sixth-graders who had already hit their growth spurt, if necessary—sit close to the door at lunch, and refrain from using the bathroom at all costs. Asher was nowhere to be seen. It was as if he had disappeared.

Theo yawned, mentally and physically exhausted. He barely heard what his sixth-hour history teacher was saying. The events of the other world competed with the fall of the Roman Empire—the other world was winning.

He didn't want to go back. He didn't want to see the Roush who'd lied to him. He didn't want to see the Shataiki, and he most definitely didn't want to meet the monster called Elyon.

He felt different, off, a bit of a zombie, maybe because of the black fog. Ruza had said he'd blinded him, but Theo could clearly see the names Romulus and Odoacer written in blue dry-erase marker on the whiteboard.

Maybe it had been a bad dream after all. He could have fallen asleep in the library, but he didn't remember falling asleep, at least not in this world. He did however remember the light. The light that transported him came from the book. If the book was the key, then the book was locked safely in the library away from Theo.

After school, Theo met his dad back where they'd parked the car. He sat on his hands, attempting to hide the gashes and burns on his wrists. He'd taken a quick glance at his reflection during third hour to see what kind of damage Asher had done to his face. Once he'd wiped the blood away, he just looked tired. His eyes were slightly blacked, but his natural coloring disguised it.

"Seat belt?" Theo's dad asked, checking the gas gauge, both side mirrors, the rearview mirror, and the driver's side mirror again.

"Check." Theo yawned.

"How was your day?"

Theo watched the passing trees, reminding himself that there were no flying creatures or beasts living in this world. "I'm alive."

His dad laughed. "Of course you are! Stayed invisible?"

"Nope." He'd said it before thinking.

"Oh?"

"No superpowers, remember?"

"You all right, buddy? You don't sound like yourself. Anything you need to talk about?"

Theo felt like he might snap. He wanted to say, *No, I'm not all right. Asher smashed my face in. I was transported to another world where I was lied to by white bats, sent on a quest by a mystic, and tortured by even larger black bats.* He wasn't all right. In fact, his mind felt heavy and foggy. He considered telling his dad what had really happened to him, but he knew his dad would never believe him. And Theo wouldn't blame him.

"Just tired," he said.

Suggesting they save their visit to the comic book shop for another day, and after takeout from their favorite Chinese restaurant, Theo asked if he could go to his room, eager to be alone.

"Sure, buddy. Are you positive that you're feeling okay?"

"It was a long day. I'm just tired."

"If you say so. I'll be in to check on you later."

Theo lumbered to his room and closed the door. He flopped down on his bed, too exhausted to change his clothes—his teeth could survive one night without brushing. He reached over and switched off his nightstand lamp, accidentally knocking his most recent issue of *The Vanisher* to the floor.

There was a split second of darkness before the sensor on his nightlight brought the room to light, exposing the shelving of hero-filled stories and epic sagas of good versus evil. Theo couldn't remember a time in his life when he had slept without light. He hated the darkness, the uncertainty, and the way his imagination conjured images of foul beasts lurking in the shadows.

Shataiki.

Theo lay on his bed. He had to think. He had to sort it all out. He had to understand. But there sat the problem: He *wasn't* able to think—not clearly. Nothing that happened in the library made sense, if in fact it had all happened while in the library. Maybe he really *had* been transported to the world of the Roush.

Think, Theo, think!

Finally, he arrived at a conclusion. None of it had happened. For all he knew, he hadn't woken up from the previous day and every bit of it—Asher, the book, the Shataiki—was a dream.

Theo's eyelids began to feel heavy. If it was a dream, he didn't want to go back to sleep. He forced his eyes open, attempting to focus on a Lego spaceship he had built in the fourth grade, but they fell shut again.

In his drowsiness Theo heard his dad enter the room, felt him place his hand upon his forehead. "Goodnight, Theo. Sleep well."

A cool breeze grazed Theo's cheek. *Who opened the window?* He reached down to pull his quilt over his head.

No blankets. No bed!

Theo opened his eyes—blue sky, water lapping on a shore in gentle waves, and behind him, desert. They'd brought him to the lake.

"No!" Theo yelled, scrambling to his feet. "No, I don't want to be here!"

Michal's green eyes widened. "But you must find Elyon, who can save—"

"You lied to me! He can't save me! If anything, he's a monster!"

They stared at him, stunned.

Theo plopped back down on the sand, wrapped his arms around his legs and tried not to cry.

A wing rested on his shoulder. Stokes settled down beside him on the sandy shoreline.

Theo ignored the Roush.

"Theo?" Stokes scooted a little closer.

"I can hear you," Theo said, annoyed.

"I failed you. If I had been stronger, none of this would have happened." Stokes sniffled, his two green eyes glistening with tears. "We will cross the lake. You will meet Elyon, and you will know he's nothing like what Ruza told you."

Theo hesitated. "I told you, I don't want to be near your Elyon. I'll stay right here until I wake up in my own bed, in my own world."

"Please, Theo. The black fog is blinding you to the truth. Elyon can help you."

Theo had had enough of their chattering on about Elyon. He jumped to his feet and stared down at Stokes. "I can see fine! I see the lake and the sand and the sky. I see my hands, and oh, look, I can see you. I see everything! I didn't ask for this!"

Michal stepped in front of Theo. "You did ask for this. Come with us and give us a chance to show you the truth. You can choose not to trust us if you want, but please let us show you Elyon. This is your quest, not ours."

He had completely forgotten about the quest for the seal—the seal that will save him from fear. The rustle of a wing at his other side startled him.

Shataiki?

He jumped back to see Gabil standing with him. His pulse quickened as memories of his time with the Shataiki invaded his thoughts. He saw the fire, the black fog, Ruza. They had given him knowledge, yet he feared them and at the same time, strangely, wanted to be with them.

He could either go with the Roush or he could sit on the beach and wait for the Shataiki to find him. What did he fear more, the Shataiki or Elyon? Theo looked out at the strange green lake, perfectly calm, like glass. He closed his eyes; the air was sweet and calming, unlike the hot stench of the Shataiki cavern.

"I know we haven't let you know much about Elyon," Michal said. "It's hard to describe the mystery of Elyon. All my words get lost when I try. He . . . he's someone you have to meet. Don't trust our words about him. Don't trust the Shataiki's words. Come with us and decide for yourself."

"It's here!" Gabil shouted, waddling toward the water. In the distance a wooden boat with a single sail floated toward the shore. It came to the edge and stopped, empty.

Theo stared at the unmanned vessel, dumbfounded. The boat had come right to them. "But how did it . . . There's no one . . ."

The mystery of Elyon.

It sounded familiar and true, but Theo decided it must be coincidence and pushed the idea aside.

Michal crawled into the boat. Gabil and Stokes followed, waiting, watching Theo. "Will you join us, Theo Dunnery?"

Theo let out the breath he'd been holding, trudged to the boat and climbed in.

Stokes met his eyes. "I'm so glad you are coming with us!"

Theo frowned and the small Roush looked confused.

The boat pushed off the sand and moved across the lake. Theo grabbed the sides, steadying himself as the vessel picked up speed. The sail caught the breeze, billowing out above the travelers. Soon they were speeding across the green water, leaving ripples in the placid lake behind them. Theo tightened his grip and made a note to add large bodies of water to the list of things he feared.

The sweet fragrance grew stronger the farther they sailed. Sunbeams bounced off the water and filled the air with a soft glow. Theo had to admit the lake was a beautiful sight. Calm settled over him as they sped across the water. The wind hummed a tune Theo could not discern. The Roush focused on something up ahead, grinning—entertained by the something Theo couldn't see. He placed his hand above his eyebrow to block the sun and squinted to see what had captivated their attention. He leaned to the left and then to the right.

Nothing.

Everything around him seemed to know something he didn't. He tried again, not wanting to miss out. Then, he felt it. Cold blackness crawling inside, keeping him from seeing what the Roush saw.

This knowledge has blinded you. And I will blind you over and over again, maggot.

Was it true? Had they blinded him? Theo didn't know what to think anymore. He wished he'd never opened that book.

Something in the sky caught his attention. A large black cloud was forming above him. Theo's eyes widened. "The fog! It's coming back for me!"

Gabil and Stokes stood to a fighting stance, rocking the boat. "I don't see anything," Stokes said.

"How can you not see it? It's right above us!"

The cloud formed a funnel that plunged down and formed a mist across the top of the water. It twirled up and around the boat, sucking Theo into its spiral.

Theo gasped for breath, suffocated by fear. The fog dug into his skin. "Help me! Help me!"

"It's fear and lies that you see," Michal cried. "Don't try to push it away; let it be. It's not really there! Don't let the lies inside of you."

"I can't! It's too strong!"

The fog consumed everything. Theo could no longer see the Roush, the boat, or the lake. All he saw was black mist surging and spinning around him. Worse, it was inside of him!

Darkness.

He couldn't move to push it back or duck to escape it. It slithered around his arms and neck like a sea of black worms, pulsing through his veins much stronger this time than the last. He screamed, but no sound came out of his mouth. It was going to take his life—he'd be gone, like his mom.

"Theo!" Gabil shouted. His voice seemed so far away. "Dive into the water. Dive into the water and let Elyon heal you!"

The water? Theo thought. *I'm afraid of the water.* But he wanted the pain to stop, and he would do anything to make it go away.

Where was the water? He couldn't see anything.

Theo struggled to push through the thick, heavy fog, found the edge of the boat, and grabbed the wood. He tugged his feet up onto the edge and used the last of his strength to dive into the water.

With a mighty splash, Theo plunged head first into the cool water, forgetting to hold his nose and close his eyes as his dad had taught him to do. A shock of pain surged and then began to subside as his body adjusted to the cold.

When he opened his eyes, he saw nothing but black. There was a sound, a boy laughing from somewhere deep in the lake—not laughing at him, but with him, as if to comfort him and tell him that everything was going to be okay.

And somehow he knew, he just knew, that the sound was his only hope, the only way to stop the pain.

Elyon?

Theo cried into the black, "Help me."

A dazzling light, golden and warm, erupted in the water. It flooded his sight and flowed through him from head to toe.

Another wave of light hit him. Theo inhaled, allowing the water to flood his mouth and lungs. The light burned, but it did not hurt. He could feel it, consuming all his fear and the pain the fear had caused.

Theo gagged as all the lies of the black fog detached from every part his body. The fog flowed from his lips, immediately absorbed by the light.

Theo willingly breathed in another lungful of light and was flooded with such incredible happiness and wonder that he began to laugh under the water.

He could think again! He could see again. He could see better, more clearly. He could see light and color everywhere he looked. He could breathe again, and he could breathe in the water.

The wonder of that moment was almost more than he could bear.

Theo wanted more—more of the sweet healing water. His anger and all of his fears were melting away. Laughing with delight, he twisted and flipped in the deep water—free of his fear, of the darkness, of the water—breathing in the colored light.

Theo.

Theo stopped his fun. He'd heard his name, but he couldn't see anyone.

Do you like what I've made for you?

Theo spun, searching for the source of the voice.

I love you, Theo.

With that, another wave of light surged up from below Theo, swallowing him in warmth that bubbled through him. He'd never felt such an overwhelming sensation of love and curiosity.

Elyon?

The light pushed Theo up, forcing him to the surface. He didn't want to leave, but he trusted the force. The light pushed him out of the water and with a mighty crash dumped him on a beach of brilliant white sand.

He was no longer in the middle of the lake but on land. Breathing hard, mind buzzing, Theo stood to his feet.

There were trees ahead, growing tall in a palette of colors—purples, reds, golds, blues—in shades he could not name. Bushy leaves of the same colors topped the trunks, dotted with fruits in a variety of shapes and sizes.

A lion roared. Theo turned, unafraid.

Judah!

On top of the massive lion sat Michal, Gabil, and Stokes—his friends, wide smiles covering their faces.

Theo smiled, allowing an unexplainable joy to wash over him.

Elyon.

He'd heard Elyon's voice. There was no doubt he'd heard it. "He loves me," Theo whispered. "He loves me!" Theo shouted and jumped to his feet.

Judah roared again, and the Roush squealed in delight. Theo kicked the sand into the air, watching it fall like snow. Dripping wet and buzzing with a happiness he'd never felt before, he was free—free of himself, free of his fears.

"Will I meet Elyon?"

Stokes nodded, as if to say, "Go ahead, climb aboard."

Judah rose, bowed his head, and waited. Needing no further encouragement, Theo jumped up on the lion's huge back, knocking the Roush onto the sand. "Oh, sorry! Sorry! I'm so sorry!"

Stokes pumped his winged fist into the air. "It's perfectly all right, son of Elyon. A little fall means nothing to me!"

Theo's heart raced. He, Theo Dunnery, was riding a lion, and he wasn't afraid! He hung tightly to Judah's mane as they sauntered along, trying to silence the questions racing through his brain. So then who was Elyon? What would he say when he got there? How would he act?

It didn't matter. He was going to meet Elyon.

Sitting atop Judah's powerful back, with the Roush following behind in silent awe, Theo looked out to the lake, replaying his dive into the water over and over—not to understand what had happened, but to recall the wonder and joy he had felt.

Judah slowed his pace. An old playground—like one Theo would have played in as a small child with a slide and swings—sat seemingly out of place on the sandy shore ahead of them.

Next to the playground stood a boy. He was a tad taller than Theo and wore a simple tunic. Even from this distance, Theo could see his brilliant blue eyes inviting him to come closer, as if they'd been friends forever and were finally meeting up again.

The Roush swooped past him and flew up to the boy. Gabil nearly tripped as he landed, wrapping his

large wings around the boy's legs. Michal took the boy's hand and lowered his head respectfully.

Stokes approached the boy timidly. He bowed before the boy, keeping his head low. The boy leaned down and kissed the top of Stokes's head. He placed his hand under the small Roush's chin and lifted it. Smiling, he wiped the tear slipping from Stokes's eye. The young Roush threw his wings around the boy, who nodded at him.

"Hello, Stokes. It's so good to meet you."

Stokes grinned from ear to ear, trembling with excitement. Then he jumped up on the slide and slid down, joined quickly by Gabil and Michal. It was strange to see the wise one—Michal—so childlike here, but seeing them flutter and hop around the swing and slide somehow made perfect sense. They were at home.

Theo slipped off Judah and walked onto the playground, looking at the boy. He was certain he'd seen those blue eyes before. Who was he?

But he knew. The boy was going to take him to Elyon. Maybe this was Elyon's son.

The boy's lips spread into a slight smile. He gestured his head to the right and headed up the beach. Theo followed immediately, picking up his pace until he was inches away from the boy's back. He wanted the boy to run, to move faster. Excitement welled inside of him. He was going to meet Elyon.

The boy walked in silence as the sounds of the Roush faded behind. Theo faithfully followed, not knowing how to voice what he wanted to say. They were on the beach, but the terrain had changed from the vast plane of sand to rolling mounds.

Finally, the boy stopped. Theo scanned the beach. Where was Elyon? The air was perfectly still;

not a sound but the gentle lapping of water could be heard.

Something's about to happen. I can feel it.

"Can I tell you a story?" the boy asked, turning to Theo.

He swallowed. "Okay."

The boy smiled, daring. "I call it show and tell." With that, he waved his hand over the sandy beach.

Theo jumped back as the sand all around them floated off the ground and swirled through the air. It clumped together, bending and twisting until Theo could clearly see its form: a lion. But it wasn't an image or a sculpture of a lion—it was totally real and alive.

"How . . .?" The word stuck in his throat.

As if to respond, the lion shook its mane and roared. Sand blew from his mouth. Theo backed away from the beast in awe.

"Lions are powerful and strong," the boy said, walking over to the lion and brushing his hand through its sandy mane. The lion rubbed against the boy, pleased.

The boy looked at Theo. "Imagine for our story that this lion is Elyon. Can you do that?"

Theo nodded. "Yes, I think so."

"Now imagine that *that*—" The boy pointed to a

dune fifty feet away. The sand swirled on the mound and a small black hyena, nearly two feet tall, sprang to life. "*That* is the enemy of Elyon."

The hyena charged at the lion, issuing a high-pitched cackle, but then stopped thirty feet away and crouched, snarling. Theo's heart hammered in his chest.

"Let's call the enemy of Elyon evil," the boy said. "So the hyena is evil. Do you understand?"

Theo nodded, still stunned by what he'd seen.

"Tell me," the boy said. "Can the hyena hurt the lion?"

Theo thought for a minute, studying the two animals. He'd learned in science that even though hyenas are much smaller, they are the lion's worst enemy because they are fast, have sharp teeth, and attack in a pack.

"Yes," Theo said. "If there are lots of them, they could easily take a lion down."

More hyenas suddenly formed out of the sand until there was a pack of eight or nine. They rushed forward and attacked the lion. The lion fought back, but in the end, he fell to the ground and sank back into the sand.

Satisfied by their kill, the hyenas retreated to the dune and faced them, waiting.

"But Elyon is much bigger than this lion," the boy said. "So let's make the lion bigger. Let's make him as big as this whole beach."

The lion appeared again, but this time it towered over Theo and the boy. He shook his mane, flinging a shower of sand down on Theo.

Incredible!

"Now," the boy said, "can the hyenas hurt the lion?"

"Yes, they can. They could bite at his heals, maybe not kill him but definitely hurt him."

Once again, the sand played out Theo's response. The hyenas raced around the lion and bit at his ankles until the great lion fell to the sand, crying out in pain.

No!

Theo hated seeing the lion in pain. The hyenas rushed back to the dune and took their place again.

"But Elyon is much, much bigger than even the lion we just saw. He's infinite."

"Infinite?"

"More powerful than anything you can ever imagine. So what if we make the lion as big as the world? What if we make it as big as all the stars and the whole universe?"

As the boy said this, the sand pulled from

underneath Theo's feet. It spread and widened, consuming the sky until suddenly Theo found himself surrounded by stars and planets. It was as if he was inside the lion—a lion as big as the universe!

Theo reached out and tried to touch the stars as they moved and danced around him. The boy stood in front of him, watching, sharing Theo's wonderment.

"Now, can those hyenas hurt the lion?"

Theo gasped. "Where are they?"

The boy pointed to a tiny planet in the far distance.

"Right where they were. They aren't infinite, so they're still the same size as before."

Theo blinked, lost in wonder. Somewhere on that tiny planet, on a beach too small for Theo to see, was a pack of hyenas. They might as well be a speck of dust compared to the lion.

"Can they hurt the lion now?" the boy asked.

"No," Theo whispered. "Never."

"Could the hyena even bother or upset the lion?"

He didn't need to answer because the answer was so obvious. Never. The hyenas, which represented everything that was against Elyon, could never bother him or upset him. How could a speck of dust threaten the lion? It was impossible.

Everything around Theo stopped as this realization fell into his mind.

"Always remember, Theo," the boy said, "that this is how powerful and big Elyon is. And the only thing bigger than Elyon's power is his love for you. Elyon is love and you are his son. The hyenas can only bother you when you forget who Elyon is and who you are as his son."

His son.

Not like he was the son of Reid and Louisa. This was different. This was more—much more. This was infinite. The stars slowly faded away, and the sand pulled back to rolling dunes. No more hyenas. No more lion. Just Theo, the boy, and the white sand in perfect calm.

Theo faced him, eyes wide. "So . . . who *is* Elyon?"

The boy grinned. "Me," he said.

Theo froze. "You?"

"I am Elyon. This body is only a form I've chosen to show you for your sake."

He . . . he'd been Elyon this whole time? This was Elyon, the infinite, showing himself to Theo in the from of a boy so that Theo could relate to him?

Theo was so overwhelmed by the idea that he impulsively fell to his knees. Tears broke from his eyes and slipped down his cheeks.

"I am so sorry. I said awful things about you. I was told you were a monster who punishes people, and I was scared."

"Most are blinded by the fog of lies and can't see who I really am," the boy said, stepping up to Theo. He sank to one knee and put his hand on Theo's shoulder. "But I've come to help you see. Do you want to see more?"

"Can I? Yes! Yes!"

The boy covered Theo's eyes with his hands then pulled them away.

"Open your eyes."

Theo slowly opened them. The world around him burst to life in new colors. The sky shown bright and golden. The lake glowed a brilliant emerald-green and glistened like sparkling jewels as it sloshed against the sugary white beach. A hum echoed around him as if creation itself was singing.

"When you have eyes to see and ears to hear, the world looks more like this than what blind eyes see," the boy said.

Theo pushed off the ground and stood in astonishment at the world around him.

"It's beautiful."

"Isn't it? Come, follow me." The boy grabbed Theo's hand.

Theo walked without hesitation, matching the boy stride for stride.

"You have the rest of your journey ahead of you—your quest," the boy said. "I'll point a finger in the right direction, but you get to take the journey yourself, yes?"

"Yes."

"Once you leave me, you'll be challenged, and it won't always be easy. You will doubt me again, more than once."

"How could I ever doubt? I never would."

"It's okay, Theo. Even when you doubt me, I love you and I'm never upset at you. Remember that as you search for the seals."

Theo tried to understand how he would ever doubt Elyon—not after what he'd seen.

The boy picked a dark stick off the sand and blew on it. The stick grew longer, twisting and intertwining until it met in a point at the top. He handed Theo what was once a simple stick but was now a staff, like a walking stick with a leather strap attached to the end. "Take this. It's a reminder of who I am and who you are. You are mine." He patted Theo's chest. "I am with you always. Remember, the only things that can threaten you are the hyenas' lies."

Theo ran his hand down the smooth wood. With the staff in his grip, he felt strong and powerful—stronger than the Shataiki, stronger than Asher, stronger than the hyenas.

"When you stand in the face of fear, you'll really know my power. The first seal will come then."

"Not now?"

The boy shook his head, smiled, and walked away. "Soon."

Theo slid the staff's strap over his shoulder and hurried after him. Judah and the Roush were waiting anxiously—the Roush sitting in the boat, wide-eyed and curious.

Theo faced the boy. "What if I fail you?"

"You can never fail me, no matter what you do. Now go, and have the same faith in yourself that I have in you."

"I will! I promise. But will I know you in the other world?"

"They call me God," the boy said.

God.

He knew that name too. "Wow!" he breathed.

"Yes, wow," the boy smiled.

Theo hugged the boy who was Elyon and who was also God, and then climbed into the boat. The boy blew and the boat pushed away from the shore as if carried by a wind even though there was no wind.

The boy on the beach quickly faded from view and was gone.

But Theo carried him in his heart, still lost in wonder.

The water seemed to sing in lush dark-green tones under the boat. Everything was brighter, clearer. Theo's cheeks hurt from smiling, but he couldn't stop. He had met Elyon—indescribable because any description would fall short, just as the Roush had said.

Overjoyed and full of boldness, Theo jumped to his feet in a fighting stance, balancing on one foot with his hands in the air. Stokes jumped back, mimicking Theo. Stokes let out a goofy *cawww* and tackled Theo. Theo fell back, laughing hysterically.

Theo popped to his feet again, hit his stance, this time motioning for Gabil. Gabil scrunched his face fiercely and lunged for Theo. Theo ducked out of the way. Gabil landed on the deck of the boat. Theo dove for Gabil. Gabil screamed as Theo landed on him in a mighty belly flop. Theo fell to the floor of the boat, clutching his stomach as he laughed hard and loud.

Michal took off to the sky, flipping and kicking. He soared upward, took a nosedive toward Theo, then swooped back up before Theo could catch him. "Even us old Roush can play too," he chuckled, plopping next to Theo on the floor.

"Elyon!" Theo cheered.

"Elyon!" echoed the Roush, his friends.

Theo had friends—brave, strong friends who deeply loved Elyon. He wanted to express how thankful he was for their friendship and help, so he leaned over the edge of the boat, scooped up a handful of green water, and stood to make a toast.

"To the love of Elyon and to you all, the Roush he sent me." Theo sipped the water from his hand. The water rushed through him, as if he had swallowed a fire that consumed every inch of his body. The three Roush quickly scooped up some water, mimicking Theo. The four travelers cheered, as Theo raised his wet palm to sky.

With an easy bump the boat finally came to a stop against the shoreline where they had camped the night before.

"What now?" Stokes asked, hopping out of the vessel.

The quest!

"I have to find the first seal. I have to really know the power of Elyon."

"We must find Talya," Michal said, leading them across the beach. "Although I think the seal may well find you before we find Talya."

"The seal will find me?" Theo said. "Elyon said I would have to stand in the face of fear."

"Exactly," Michal said.

Facing his fears was the way to the first seal, that much was now plain, but knowing this didn't dampen his enthusiasm. He'd seen Elyon's infinite power and he had the staff.

But as they traveled farther from the waters of Elyon, Theo noticed the colors around him fading back to their normal hues. They weren't as vivid and as beautiful as before. In fact, his new sense of peace and power had faded too. What if his courage faded as well? What if it eventually faded completely away?

The landscape shifted as they journeyed; walls of rock towered high above them. A twinge of Theo's former anxiety emerged. "I don't remember this being here, Michal."

"We took you around the perimeter when you were asleep. It will be much quicker to climb and cut through the middle of the canyon. Do you think you can manage?"

The jagged cliff loomed above them.

Heights.

"I'll fly next to you, Theo," Stokes said. "I'll protect you."

Stokes had said that once before.

Theo nodded. Using the staff of Elyon, he pulled himself up on a rock, then to another and another. He climbed higher, easier than he had assumed. The Roush flew in close proximity, keeping with his pace.

It took nearly all of his strength and a few small slips, but he was almost at the top. One more ledge to go. Theo grabbed the edge and pulled himself up, but as he did, his fingers began to slip. "Michal, help!"

Silence.

The staff of Elyon dangled on his wrist. It was slipping.

Don't let go.

Theo flung his free hand up and caught the edge of the cliff. He dug his fingernails into the rock and wriggled his feet until the tips of his Converse were securely on something.

A squeal and thump sounded behind him. "Michal? Gabil? Stokes?"

No response.

Theo pulled with every ounce of strength within him. Where were his protectors when he needed them?

At the top, the sight of what waited beyond the wall crashed into him. Hundreds of Shataiki filled the canyon—the walls and ground were lined with them. A shrill shriek echoed below as one of the bats caught sight of Theo. The others followed in a contagion of raucous squawking. Ruza and Shax stood in the middle of it all, sinister smiles etched on their black faces.

Theo spun to find the Roush, but they were gone. Panicked, he scanned the area around him, and then he saw them, all three, in the clutches of the Shataiki. The Roush were warriors, his protectors. They must have been so focused on not letting him fall that they didn't see the Shataiki coming.

Theo watched in horror as the Shataiki tied the Roush to heavy stakes. At their feet the Shataiki placed piles of wood. They were going to burn his friends!

"No!"

Theo scrambled down the cliff, sliding on loose pebbles, scraping the exposed skin on his arms and ripping his jeans. He had to save them!

Shataiki swooped close in behind him—he could

feel their wings beating the air inches from his head. One landed on him and licked his neck, and when he tried to shake it free, its claws cut down his back.

The leather strap holding the staff Elyon had given him snapped. The staff clattered down the hill. He didn't have time to think about it much less go after it. It was all he could do to ignore the pain in his back.

Screaming, he spun and slugged the Shataiki onto its backside, finally knocking it free. But in the process, he tripped and tumbled to the bottom of the steep hill.

"Theo!" Stokes cried. The Roush fought against the ropes that bound him, but it was no use.

Pain screamed through Theo's body. He could feel the blood seeping into his T-shirt as the scrapes on his back oozed.

Ruza approached him slowly, chuckling. "Poor little human. You had the chance to listen to me, but you chose to be brainwashed by the lies of Elyon."

Black fog once again slipped from the beast's lips and drifted toward Theo.

"Sadly, you and your friends must now die. Elyon can't save you. Why would he? Look at you, Theo. You're such a disappointment to him."

Theo struggled to his feet, head spinning. "You

are the one who lies, Ruza!" he yelled. His voice bounced through the canyon. "Elyon isn't the monster you told me he was!"

Ruza stared at him, disgusted. He suddenly launched himself forward, a streaking slash of black fur, claws extended.

Theo dove to his right and rolled out of reach. He came to a crouch and saw Elyon's staff a few feet away.

Ruza was circling back around, rushing him already. Frantic, Theo dove for the staff, grabbed it with his right hand, and swung it up like a baseball bat just as Ruza reached him.

The staff slammed into the Shataiki's face. Ruza screeched as he fell to the ground.

Furious now, he lunged to his feet and charged toward Theo. Ruza slashed at Theo's jaw with his claw, grazing it enough to make him wince with pain. Before the beast could slash again, Theo swung the staff with all his might. It cracked Ruza's jaw and the bat flew backward, flailed wildly, and landed with a thud.

Theo didn't take the time to think or wait for the Shataiki to collect itself. He spun and ran.

"Get him!" Ruza screamed.

With a terrible shriek, a hundred black bats

launched themselves at him from every direction. Theo took a sharp turn and pumped his feet as fast as they'd go. A Shataiki caught him from behind and dragged a claw across Theo's arm. Two more nipped at his back.

Theo ran faster, blind with fear.

There was no way to fight them off—or save his friends. But he had to try to at least escape, or he'd never get the seal.

Theo reached the incline and scrambled up as fast as he could, doing his best to swat at the Shataiki with the staff as they nipped at him. He reached the top much quicker than expected, but the sky was now full of the flying beasts, and there was nowhere to run. The other side was way too steep!

There was no hope!

Mind now lost in fear, Theo closed his eyes tight and desperately tried to think of Elyon. The moment he imagined the boy, the world around him slowed. The shrieks of the Shataiki faded, and the hot, thick air became motionless and cool.

Who am I, Theo?

Theo's heart jumped. He'd heard Elyon's gentle voice. "You are Elyon," he said aloud. "You are infinite."

And who are those who come against me?

Theo recalled the boy's story about the lion and the hyenas. "The hyenas," he said. "Shataiki!"

Can they hurt me?

"No."

Can they threaten me?

"No."

And where am I?

"With me. Everywhere."

Closer than your breath. So why do you fear, my son?

Theo blinked. He'd forgotten!

Since I'm with you, what can threaten you?

Theo knew. He knew for certain in that moment and he shouted it for all to hear.

"Nothing! Nothing can threaten me, because you are all powerful. You are the light without darkness. You are infinite. Nothing can threaten you, so nothing can threaten me."

Now open your eyes, Theo. Show them who I am.

Theo opened his eyes and saw the Shataiki moving in slow motion. He looked at the staff in his hand and then back up at the Shataiki. This was Elyon's staff and he was Elyon's son. So what hope did the black beasts have?

None.

Theo placed both hands on the staff, raised

it above his head, and slammed it down into the ground.

"Elyon is the light!" Theo roared at the top of his lungs. "Nothing can threaten him!"

Light erupted from the bottom of the staff. It streamed into the sky and flooded the canyon.

He could feel the power of Elyon surging through the staff, through his arms, through his entire body.

The Shataiki shrieked and fled before the blazing light, but it was too late. Like drawings made of nothing but imagination, they popped and vanished into wisps of black fog as the light touched them. In one moment, hundreds of Shataiki had filled the canyon; in the next, they were gone, like vanished shadows.

The light slowly drew back into the staff in Theo's hands as he stared in amazement. Something tingled on his left shoulder, under his shirt, something hot.

He dropped the staff and jerked up his sleeve. The same light that had come from the staff now glowed under his skin in the form of a circle, like the one on the door Talya had sent him through. But now that seal was on Theo's arm. It was like a tattoo, but it was made of light instead of ink. It was under his skin, glowing, on the arm of Elyon's son.

I am the light. Nothing can threaten me.

"White," he said aloud. "Elyon is the light; nothing can threaten him."

And with those words, he knew that he had found the first seal.

Theo heard sounds of cheers coming from below. He hurried to the edge. There, below, were the three Roush, tied up, shouting in celebration. He quickly climbed down to free his friends.

"Did you see that?" Theo asked, breathless as he ran toward them.

"We saw!" Gabil said.

Theo tugged at the knots securing the ropes. He pulled and unloosed them, effortlessly freeing the Roush.

"Theo has vanquished the Shataiki!" Gabil cried.

And more, he had found the first seal.

Stokes bounced over to Theo and lifted his sleeve. The white circle continued to glow on his skin. "Wow!"

"I knew you could do it," Michal said, dipping his head in respect.

"You, Theo, are now the master of the great fighting arts," Gabil said with a quick punch to the air. "The student is now the teacher. Although, I must say, you never actually let me teach you."

Theo had stood in the face of the Shataiki—the fears that battered him—and had found the first of the five seals.

Elyon is infinite and cannot be threatened by anything, ever.

A roar filled the canyon. Theo spun to the sound. "Judah?" He searched the canyon for the lion and then saw him standing at the opening of the canyon.

"Judah!"

Theo raced toward his furry friend. The Roush took to the air, hot on his heels. When he reached Judah, he threw his arms around the lion's massive furry neck. Judah shuddered but let Theo hold him tight.

Talya stepped forward from the side cliff and approached them, watching Theo attentively. Theo released Judah and returned the old man's smile. He pulled up his sleeve, revealing the glowing seal on his shoulder.

Talya's chuckle echoed softly through the canyon. He stepped up to Theo, knelt to one knee and ruffled his hair.

"Son of Elyon, you have done it. The first seal. You are a brave boy, Theo Dunnery." Talya rose. "Now let me see your staff."

Theo handed it to him. Talya examined the finely crafted walking stick. He drew his long fingers along the smooth wood, as if he knew a secret about the staff that Theo didn't.

"Very nice. Reminds me of mine." He handed back the staff and walked over to the Roush. "My dear little friends, you've done a magnificent job. Michal and Gabil, good work as always."

Gabil and Michal gave him a little bow.

"And you, Stokes, were certainly most impressive. You might find yourself on many quests with young Theo."

He faced Theo. "This quest is done, but there are four more seals to be found if you are to completely conquer your fear."

"But I'm not afraid anymore! I faced the hyenas! I defeated the Shataiki! I know who I am."

Talya's brow cocked. "Do you? Until you have all five, the others can easily be lost. Find all five and your life will never be the same."

"Lose it? You mean the white circle can disappear?"

"Indeed. In the fog of life, it is quite easy to forget

what you learn. And if you forget, the seal will vanish. But don't worry about it. When the time comes I will send a sign for you."

"Sign for what?"

"For you to return and resume your quest, naturally."

"What kind of sign?"

"One you won't be able to mistake. And so you know, for the next quest, you will need to bring someone with you from your world."

Theo thought about that. He didn't really have any friends.

"How will I know who to bring?"

"Perhaps it would be better if they aren't your friend. Don't worry, you will know who to bring when the time comes."

The thought made his stomach turn, but he quickly pushed the concern away, exchanging it for a truth. He did have friends—Michal, Gabil, and Stokes.

But they were in his dreams. Or were they?

"Yes and no," Talya said with a smile. "It's time to say your goodbyes, Theo. We will be seeing you very soon, so don't be too sad."

Theo nodded and turned to embrace his friends. "Thank you. I couldn't have ever done this without you."

"It was an honor," Michal said.

"You are very special, my friend," Gabil said with his ginormous grin.

"I will miss you, Theo, and I will be eagerly waiting for our next adventure to begin!" Stokes hugged Theo once more.

A sudden and unexpected eagerness to return home overcame Theo. "Talya, I'm ready."

Talya lifted his hand, placed two fingers on Theo's forehead and pushed. "Soon, son of Elyon."

The world around Theo began to disappear. Then it was black and empty. He immediately felt as if he was emerging from a deep sleep—a dream, but more than a dream. Theo opened his eyes, He was in his room, staring at the ceiling fan.

He was home.

Theo could hear the bustling sounds of his dad in the kitchen—the pop of the toaster and the gurgle of the coffee pot. He sat up quickly and rubbed his eyes. The last thing he remembered was going to bed early, but now it was morning. More time had passed this visit, and his whole night was gone.

Had it really happened? His sheets were pulled up over his body and the comic book he had knocked off rested neatly on his nightstand. *Dad must have done it in the middle of the night.* So, he hadn't left

his bed. He had been here and in the other world at the same time—asleep in one and awake in another. Was it possible?

There was one way to know for sure.

Theo jerked up the sleeve of his T-shirt. The white circle glowed in the dimly lit room.

Theo let out a quiet laugh and dropped back on his pillow. "Yes! Yes! Yes!"

It had happened. All of it. And he wanted to go back. But how? Did he have to fall asleep or would he need the book?

Theo jumped out of bed and paced his room. Talya said he'd have to bring someone back, possibly someone from school. Who would he bring? Would they be able to see Elyon?

Elyon.

Theo stopped, closed his eyes, and breathed in the memory. He knew Elyon was with him in this very moment, but to be in his presence again, that's what Theo wanted.

"Theo, come on, time to go," his dad yelled from the bottom of the stairs.

No time to shower.

Theo tossed his dirty clothes into his closet, pulled on a plain black T-shirt, clean boxers, socks, a pair of jeans, and his Converse.

He took one last look around his room. The nightlight glowed in the corner—The Vanisher staring past him.

"I'm not afraid," he said, unplugging the nightlight and slipping it into his dresser drawer. Darkness was merely another hyena—a fear that he had overcome.

Theo dashed to the bathroom, squeezed mint toothpaste on his toothbrush, and brushed. He spat, rinsed, and brushed again, catching a glimpse of his reflection. A deep red scratch marred his lower cheek.

He stopped brushing mid-stroke. The scratch from Ruza! Whatever happened to his body in the other world also happened here, which meant the scratches on his back from his fall were probably also there. How would he explain them to his dad?

A twinge of pain shot through his cheek as he recalled the moment the bat's claw connected with his jaw. He heard a whisper, the crackling of the Shataiki: *Fear us.*

Theo smirked, replacing that thought with another: *I, Theo, son of Elyon, fear nothing.*

He spat into the sink, washed out his toothbrush, opened the medicine cabinet and grabbed a Band-Aid to cover the scratch. Then he pulled his sleeve up on his shoulder to see the white seal on his arm. *Still there.*

Theo hurried down the stairs and into the kitchen where his dad was putting the finishing touches on their lunches—peanut butter and jelly.

"There you are. I was worried you were playing sick again."

"Nope, overslept, I guess."

His dad dropped the jelly-smeared knife and hurried to his son. "What happened to your face? I didn't notice it when I tucked you in. Are you okay?"

"What?"

"The Band-Aid."

Theo reached up and touched the latex strip. "Oh! This. I'm fine, really. It doesn't hurt. It's . . ." He knew his dad would think he had gone crazy if he told the truth.

Elyon, help me.

"It must have happened last night while I slept." Truth.

"Well, make sure you cut your nails before bed tonight. Okay, buddy?"

"Okay, Dad."

His dad glanced at Theo's exposed shoulder. He'd forgotten to pull his sleeve back down. Could his dad see the white circle on his arm? This one he couldn't explain away.

"Dad, there's something—"

"Pull your sleeve down, buddy."

His dad couldn't see the seal? No. But it was real. Incredible.

"I've packed our lunches, and Pop-Tarts are ready to go. Are you ready for the day?"

Theo grinned and pulled down his sleeve. "I'm more than ready."

Theo, son of Elyon, Shataiki slayer.

And it was all just beginning.

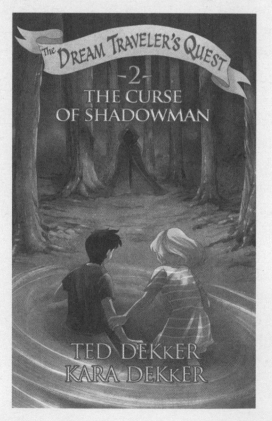

CONTINUE THE QUEST!

THE DREAM TRAVELER'S QUEST

-2-

THE CURSE OF SHADOWMAN

TED DEKKER
KARA DEKKER